Also by Rick Brown and Reg Cox

The X-odus Files: Following God in an Alien Land

ME
ADDICTION

having it my way isn't so great after all

Rick Brown, Reg Cox,
Jer Villanueva, Dr. Glen Villanueva

WestBow
PRESS
A DIVISION OF THOMAS NELSON

Blessings to you in your walk with the Lord ~

WestBow Press books may be ordered through booksellers or by contacting:

WestBow Press
A Division of Thomas Nelson
1663 Liberty Drive
Bloomington, IN 47403
www.westbowpress.com
1-(866) 928-1240

Because of the dynamic nature of the Internet, any web addresses or links contained in this book may have changed since publication and may no longer be valid. The views expressed in this work are solely those of the author and do not necessarily reflect the views of the publisher, and the publisher hereby disclaims any responsibility for them.

Certain stock imagery © Thinkstock.
Any people depicted in stock imagery provided by Thinkstock are models, and such images are being used for illustrative purposes only.

Scripture quotations are from *The Holy Bible, English Standard Version*, copyright © 2001 by Crossway Bibles, a publishing ministry of Good News Publishers. Used by permission. All rights reserved.

ISBN: 978-1-4497-3031-4 (hc)
ISBN: 978-1-4497-3030-7 (sc)
ISBN: 978-1-4497-3029-1 (e)

Library of Congress Control Number: 2011919408

Printed in the United States of America

WestBow Press rev. date: 11/10/2011

Need pampering? This isn't the book. Ready for some healthy, balance-giving perspective? You'll find it in these pages.

—Max Lucado, pastor and bestselling author

This book shouts the solution to a troubled self serving nation of Me-addicts. They really need this book. Ok. Fine. WE really need this book!

—Your friend and mine, Bob Smiley, Comedian,
www.bobsmiley.com

This powerful book serves as a mirror that Christians have long avoided gazing into. In its pages you will see your "Me Addicted" reflection which has kept you from being all that God intended. As you read, you will be challenged to change your addiction, transform your faith, and revolutionize your impact on the world.

—Christie Love, Executive Director of LeadHer,
www.leadher.org

This book grabbed me in the first paragraph, and wouldn't let go—even after I had turned the last page. It is crammed with humor. But it is deadly serious. Here Rick Brown hits the bull's-eye of the human soul. No. *ME Addiction* is not a "religious" book. Rather it's about raw, red-blooded reality. Read on if you have the nerve.

—Lynn Anderson, author and founder of Mentor Network,
www.mentornetwork.org

This is a sound, well thought through read that challenges the status quo of always thinking of myself first. It is both entertaining and thought provoking. Because no one is immune from self-focused thinking and behavior, this book pierces you in the heart. You will find yourself pondering this book's message for a long time after finishing it.

—Phil Schubert, EdD, President,
Abilene Christian University

In *ME Addiction*, Rick Brown (and company) does the thing I fear the most . . . he made me look honestly at my pride and self-centeredness and call it what it is. Brown has a way of sucking me in with compelling stories, lightening the mood with his hilarious way of expressing himself, then socking it to me with brutal truthfulness. This is a great book that helped me actually do something about at least a few of my addictive ME-oriented habits.

—Shelley Leith, co-author, Character Makeover and creator of 40 Days of Purpose Campaign

This book has *ME* written all over it! When I live by the positive principles outlined, it brings out the best in me. Additionally, as a general rule, it also brings out the best in others around me. However, sometimes the negative *me* gets in the way and I need to be reminded to live for a cause greater than myself. Thanks *ME Addiction* for that very authentic reminder and a biblically-grounded game plan to live by.

—Dr. Jimmy Sites, TV Producer & Host: www.SpiritualOutdoorAdventures.org

To the ME Addiction team,
whose meeting in Rio Vista
birthed the contents of this book.
May we all continue to be
ME-free
and
God-addicted.

Contents

Foreword

Two years ago, I was introduced to Shoestring Ministries and Dr. Glen Villanueva by a mutual friend, comedian Bob Smiley. They invited me to perform in a four-city Northern California concert-type tour called the *Me-addiction Tour.* "Tour? Sure! I'd be happy to, but . . . Me-addiction? What's that all about?"

After talking to Glen a time or two, I realized his passion and the message of Shoestring Ministries was fairly simple and clear: challenge and encourage people to be less self-focused and more Jesus focused. Whoa! I could get behind something like that. And so I did.

Eating dinner late one night after one of the concerts, we talked about writing books and producing music. As I explained that night, I've written music meant for a small number of folks, like a boutique album, and I have also made other albums intended for popular consumption, for the masses, like much of the music I did when I was with the Newsboys. The same is true for books, and this one definitely falls into the latter category. This book is not for just a few people. It is a powerful read meant for the masses. And that includes you!

This is a book we've all been wanting but didn't know we needed. It helps us answer a question we didn't even know we were being asked:

"Where are we?"

It's the first question God asked Adam, who was hiding in the bushes after eating the forbidden fruit. Well, I'm guessing when Adam heard God walking through the garden calling, "Where are you, Adam?" (Genesis 3:9), he knew he was in a bad spot. He'd been deceived so greatly that when faced with the reality of his situation, all he could do was make weak excuses and lie.

The fact is, God knew exactly where Adam was and what he had been a part of. All God wanted was for Adam to be still and take stock of the situation and give an honest account. It's the same for us today. God knows exactly where we are and how we got here.

Many of us claim to be followers of Jesus, yet we still find ourselves with an insatiable appetite and thirst for more. We fill our time, minds and stomachs with more, more, and still more. Yet we find ourselves unsatisfied. Why? Because we've become a ME-centric people and we don't even know how it happened.

One of Shoestring Ministries t-shirts says in big letters: "Help Stop the ME Addiction" across the chest. It's a shirt so bold you can't ignore it. Since the tour, I've worn this t-shirt while running errands, shopping, doing everyday-life stuff. This shirt has been met with confusion—and stares!—followed by the hesitant question, "Umm, excuse me, what's your shirt mean?" My answer starts out superficial but then it often dives into deeper conversation.

It gives me a chance to unravel the movement started in California by a small band of Christ followers called to challenge people to be different, to move the center of the universe off of me and on to Christ, where it belongs. The message allows an opening for personal testimony and to ask people, "Aren't you tired of being like the rest of the world?" After all, it really isn't about me or us, is it? It's about HIM!

In the high speed, media-centered, consumer-driven society in which we live, God calls us to slow down long enough to bring clarity to our minds and bring satisfaction to our souls. This book helps clear our heads and cut through the malaise of the cultural and personal deception of "ME first!"

This book is really cool and we know you're going to be blown away by it! You, your motives, and priorities will be challenged to the core of your being, straight to your heart, so be ready.

Let the revolution of change continue!

Phil & Heather Joel
Founders of deliberatePeople,
www.deliberatepeople.com

Acknowledgments

Writing a book is a monumental task, and it has taken the effort and influence of many to get to the finish line. Our gratitude runs deep.

Rick would like to thank:

Glen Villanueva for inviting me into the ME Addiction team and for this opportunity to write.

Reg, Jer, and Paul for their input in how this book would take shape.

Denny Boultinghouse for his editorial skill and helpful suggestions that made this a better book.

ChristBridge Fellowship for being Jesus together in our community.

Lynn Anderson for a lifetime of mentoring and for his encouragement to rewrite the last chapter.

My sons Kristofer and Taylor who have become young men that make their father proud.

Jenn, our first daughter-in-law, for bringing more beauty into our family.

And to Karen my wife: the Borghese has Bernini but God gave me his masterpiece of you. Let's go another twenty-five.

Reg would like to thank:

I'm indebted to friends and family who have put up with my lifelong "me addiction" and have invested in my heart.

My wife Amy, my kids Levi and Faith Ann, my parents, friends the Villanuevas, Maldonados, Browns, Roberts, and the many others who loved me as God transformed my character.

Jer would like to thank:

Glen Villanueva for unwavering dedication and energy that helped complete this project along with the *What's in it for Him* ministry team of Yvonne, Paul, and Sarah.

Reg Cox and Rick Brown for insight, humor, and feedback.

Milton Jones for sharing a passion for the gospel of Jesus and training me in my early ministry and your continuing influence to this day.

Mom and Dad for modeling God's faithfulness, charity, and grace.

My children, Sydney, Elias, and Noelle. You are God's precious gifts and I am blessed to be your father. And for my wife Lyn—the journey is not always easy, but you keep me grounded, inspire me to think deeper, and support me unconditionally. There's no one else I would rather share this adventure with.

Glen would like to thank:

Mom and Dad for showing me committed lifelong faith and service to God.

Bella and Jerry Maldonado for loving me not as a son-in-law, but a son.

Rick Brown for leading the charge on this project and my brother Jer for writing the initial manuscript that laid the foundation for this book.

Reg Cox and Kevin Roberts for a kinship and brotherhood that extends past the ordinary into the life-changing.

Paul and Sarah Sale for jumping in with both feet to birth, develop, and grow Shoestring Ministries, as together we follow God's lead.

The Shoestring crew of core volunteers and consultants (Monica Baker, Chris and Cindy Fox, Bill Kuenzinger, Maxine Louis, Wayne and Sheila Smith, Ginger and Alan Stark) for all your behind-the-scenes work.

My brothers at Pinnacle Forum, especially Chuck Bryant, for your prayers, understanding, and wisdom.

Randy Zachary for encouragement, friendship and vision to impact the Kingdom via radio and our collective influence.

My daughters Maya and Ani for being patient with me all those evenings as I worked on this project. I love you both so much I can't even put a number on it!

And to my beautiful wife and constant support, Yvonne. You had no idea what you were getting into when you said yes, but I'm sure glad you did. Much love to you for laughing, sharing and walking beside me in this unpredictable life of ours.

Introduction

I've noticed a disturbing trend in the world (and yes, even in churches!) over the last few years. Maybe you have, too? You can see it in everyday life: people behaving in increasingly self-centered ways.

- The child who repeatedly throws a tantrum in the store because he can't have what he wants. And the parents who buy it anyway because they'd rather keep him quiet than provide him with discipline and guidance.
- The dad who chooses time with the guys and hobbies over his family and then wonders why his kids don't want to be with him.
- A family spending their time buried in electronics instead of communicating with each other.
- Individuals posting videos of themselves doing provocative, dangerous, or bizarre activities to sites like YouTube in hopes of being seen by millions.

This idea of self-focus hit close to home with me a few years ago when a good friend left his wife and children after nearly two decades of marriage. He was a Christ follower, a church leader, and a man who loved God and his family. When his wife tried to understand the reasons for his leaving, she heard him say: "Our marriage isn't working for me," "You're just not meeting my needs," and "This isn't what I envisioned for my life."

You can change the details, circumstances, and names, but you know this couple. You've served alongside them at youth rallies, worked together on service projects, raised your children with theirs, and had them over for dinner. And you've likely seen or experienced the aftermath of this relationship implosion.

What struck me was that his reasons loudly echoed the world's mantra of "What's in it for me?"

Churches are encountering a more "me-centric" shift in their ministry efforts. People aren't serving unless it's convenient. Classes don't have teachers because it's too much of a time commitment. Volunteers are hard to come by because of soccer practice, music lessons, long hours at work, overcommitted schedules, you name it. It's a variation on a theme; one you're probably familiar with.

The more I looked around, the more I got discouraged. And then I got mad. Why? Because this isn't what God meant for us. It's not supposed to be this way! As I fumed, it occurred to me that Christ followers are asking the wrong question. Instead of asking "What's in it for me?", we need to ask, *"What's in it for Him?"*

When frustrated, we too easily throw our hands up in the air and say, "Oh well, I can't do anything about it." Not this time. I didn't want to stand back or lay down while watching the world's attitudes and priorities encroach more and more into the fiber and fabric of God's people. Out of a desire to do something about this growing problem, Shoestring Ministries was born. With my wife, Yvonne, and good friends Paul and Sarah Sale, we formed this ministry around one simple vision: *Mindset, attitude, and behavior change by taking the focus off of me and putting it on Christ.*

With committed prayer, the tireless efforts and generosity of many, and of course, praise and honor to God who has done *all* of the heavy lifting, Shoestring Ministries is making progress to stem the tide against the misguided idea that the world revolves around "me." The world doesn't revolve around me or you. It never has and never will. It revolves around the one true God and Jesus Christ, our Savior.

We are humbled and honored to be a part of this book and its message. Our collective prayer is that, after reading it, you will share this book with others and live a life closer to what God intended, one with less of me and more of Him.

Dr. Glen A. Villanueva
CEO & Co-founder, Shoestring Ministries, Inc.
shoestringministries.org
facebook.com/wiifh

Chapter 1

A ME-Free World

Let's get our cards out on the table first thing. What if I told you that you and I are addicted? That we spend a fair amount of time thinking about ourselves: what makes *us* happy, what *we* want, what makes *us* feel good? Simply put, *you and I* think the world revolves around *us*.

Before you deny that you have an addiction, you might note that denial is a defense mechanism in many addicts. At first, I denied the addiction, too. I understand, so stay with me for a bit. You see, our addiction is the oldest addiction.

The people in Ptolemy's second-century world had it, too. Ptolemy believed that Earth was the center of the universe. Can't blame him. If you watch the sun and moon and stars, it looks as if they are taking a never-ending trip around our little sphere.

For years, Ptolemy's astronomical theories went unchallenged. It's easy to understand why. You see, if the Earth was the center of the universe, then humans were at the center of the universe. It's a nice thought. We are so important that even the heavenly bodies plan their journeys around us, probably hoping to catch a glimpse of the important things we are doing like eating pizza and walking the dog and zoning out with iPods.

Ptolemy's ideas were so well liked that they lasted for several hundred years—years of people believing that everything revolved around them. Day after day, people thought that everything in this world existed for them.

Until Copernicus came along one day. He believed that it was not the Earth but the sun that maintained the center position in our universe. Copernicus had written about this as early as 1514, but he remained quiet for fear of scorn from others in the scientific community. He finally relented and had his ideas published in a book.

About a hundred years later, Galileo supported the work of Copernicus. It landed him in house arrest for the remainder of his life.

Few today would dare say that Ptolemy had it right, even though for hundreds of years no one offered a challenge. Challenging the common thinking of the day can be risky.

I'm feeling a bit risky today. There is an addiction that has taken hold of us all: the ME–addiction. It's thinking that "I am the center of the universe," that everything revolves around "me," and that in everything you do, the primary question to ask is *"What's in it for me?"*

The ME-addiction. That's what Ptolemy had. That's what I had. And so do you. What? You don't think so? Ptolemy did not think there was any way he could be seeing things wrongly, either, until Copernicus came along and began meddling into the flow of the universe, asking questions and challenging the status quo.

It's a good thing he did. With the sun as the center of the universe, planets and other orbs fell into their proper place. The world was righted.

You probably sense that your world needs to be righted, too, that it's not as it's supposed to be. Do you really think God created you to suffer from doubt? From anxiety? From fear? From addictions? You know the answer to those questions. Those things are not good. But everything God created was good.

Maybe you need a look at what a ME-free world once looked like, so let's go back in time.

Not just to the days of your childhood. Yes, it was an innocent age. That season of life where you knew nothing of real sin. You had no responsibilities weighing you down. You had time to lie on the summer grass and watch the clouds float by in shapes of animals and objects that only your imagination could see.

Not just to your first day on your first job. Minimum wage made you feel like a millionaire. Seeing your name in lights—well, at least on a name tag—caused a pride to swell inside of you. No mistakes made yet. No hopes dashed. Just a bright future ahead.

Not just to the day of your wedding. Oh, how everything was magical. The girls lined up in Cinderella dresses like something right out of a fairytale. The guys leaving their T-shirts and tattered jeans behind for tuxes. Everyone smiling. You and your betrothed had no problems and much passion and you believed the unity candle would never burn out.

Not just to the first day as a mother or father. You had made no parenting mistakes. Spoken no cross words. Your child had uttered no back talk, only baby talk. That little pair of eyes lit up when you walked in the room.

But now you are weary from a life marred by sin. Your job is mundane. You marriage is boring or broken. Your children's eyes only light up when you leave the room or hand them money.

Who wouldn't want a different world? So let's go further back than your childhood or first day on the job. Let's go to the book of beginnings, the book of Genesis. "In the beginning, God . . ."[1] The simplicity simply astounds. These words were written not as a heady scientific explanation but as a heart-filled expression of faith. There was a beginning to the story of our lives.

And at that beginning, it is worth noting that God was there. Students of grammar quickly diagram the words and find their subject. In the very first line in the very first sentence of all of Scripture, at the very start of the story designed to tell you about your life, you make the most important discovery you will ever find: the subject from the very beginning has always been God! It is not you. It is not "me." God gets center-stage attention from the get-go.

Once you find your subject, you know it is followed by a verb, at least in a well crafted sentence it is. And we find one: "In the beginning, God *created* . . ."[2] This is no God that stands on the sidelines and watches but one who is active and involved.

The word *create* means to give shape to something. Kids create on a much lower level when they take a lump of Play-Doh and fashion it into the shape of an animal. Beach lovers get more extravagant when they take sand and build elaborate sandcastles.

But God can create both out of nothing and out of things that exist. He can even take chaos and give it order and form. Let's get back to diagramming. We have a subject: God. We have a verb: created. When you look for a direct object, you find what he created: the heavens and the earth. But it's in the next line that you find chaos. "The earth was without form and void, and darkness was over the face of the deep."[3]

You may have thought the beginning would be a neatly packaged, perfect setting, a far cry from a description of what you experience on a daily basis. Surprisingly, the beginning may sound more like your present life than you think: "Without form and void."

That's the ME-addicted world we live in: "Without form and void." It's the life that has no shape, no substance. It's the world we want to get away from at times.

Like we did recently. My wife and I went to an all-inclusive resort in a paradise called Jamaica. It seemed as if we had been put down right in the middle of the garden of Eden: beautiful beach, endless buffet of food, and abundant produce.

Speaking of produce, one of the first Jamaicans we met introduced himself as "the Farmer." He immediately displayed for me a sample of his crop. It was home-grown and home-packaged in a zip-lock bag and looked a little like green tea. Since we had all the food we needed, I declined his offer and bought a beaded necklace from him instead.

It was a week in which stress was left behind: no bills to pay, no deadlines to meet, only an opportunity to commune with God, nature and each other.

But then the week ended. We wound up sitting on a plane in Montego Bay that was going nowhere. The pilot informed us that a piece of polyurethane inside one of the engines had peeled up and they had to repair it or else our flight might be fatal. I was suddenly glad we were sitting on the tarmac rather than flying. About an hour later all was pronounced "good" and off we went.

As soon as we arrived back home we could feel it again: the things that needed to be done, the concern about projects, the relational tensions—back to a world "without form and void."

But for a moment we had a taste of what could be.

And for a moment, we can go back to the beginning and get a taste of what is meant to be. The God who created the heavens and the earth and shaped chaos into his creation still creates today. Listen to the words of this picture from the ME-free world:

> And the Lord God planted a garden in Eden, in the east, and there he put the man whom he had formed. And out of the ground the Lord God made to spring up every tree that is pleasant to the sight and good for food. The tree of life was in the midst of the garden, and the tree of the knowledge of good and evil. [4]

That world was lost when the ME-addiction began. We'll see that soon enough. For now, trust that God is working to bring back this new world. His desire is to make something new again. He created in the beginning, and he is creating now. Notice the words of Paul in Ephesians 2:10: "For we are his workmanship, created in Christ Jesus for good works, which God prepared beforehand, that we should walk in them."

The word used for *workmanship* is the same Greek word used to translate the Hebrew *created* in Genesis 1:1. It's the same word used to describe the careful, thoughtful, passionate work of a poet. You and I are God's poems; his creations.

Once a creator, always a creator. God is in the business of taking lives that are chaotic and without form and shaping them into something new. He fashions them into creations for good works.

And he does all of this in his son Christ Jesus. Don't you think that a God who could create the heavens and the earth, and take an earth that was in chaos and create order, could also create something new in you?

Some of the closing words of the Bible mirror the opening ones. John, the exiled apostle, keeps writing scenes of what he is seeing from God. He says, "Then I saw a new heaven and a new earth . . . the river of the water of life . . . the tree of life . . ."[5]

Is that a vision of life you'd like for your own? Then do as did the writer of Genesis. Put God as the subject of your life. Follow the example of Copernicus. Put the Son at the center of your universe.

And see if your world doesn't begin to spin a little better.

Chapter 2

The Reason for Being

The idea was drummed up by the *Washington Post* as a social experiment: Place a violinist in a subway playing some beautiful classical music and see what happens. But no ordinary violinist would be secured. Instead, the violinist would be Joshua Bell, an internationally acclaimed virtuoso.[1]

And no ordinary violin would be played. Instead, Bell would serenade his subway audience with a 1713 Stradivarius that cost him about $3.5 million.

And it would be no ordinary music he played. Instead, he would play selections from Bach to "Ave Maria." What many would cough up one hundred dollars just to sit in the cheap seats to hear, people that morning—for forty-five minutes—would get to hear for free.

Wearing jeans, a long-sleeved t-shirt, and a baseball cap, Bell entered the L'enfant Plaza metro station in Washington DC on January 12, 2007 at 7:51 a.m. He pulled out his violin, put a few coins and dollars in his open violin case as seed money, and began to play.

Three minutes went by before the first person stopped and looked as if they even noticed Bell. Sixty-three people had already passed him by. A half-minute later he got his first donation: a one dollar bill. Joshua played for forty-five minutes. In that time, seven people stopped moving for at least a minute to hang around and listen to the music. A whopping twenty-seven gave money as they scurried by, for a grand total of thirty-two dollars and some change. That left 1,070 people who hurried past him oblivious to the grandness that was only a few feet away. Few even turned to look.

I wonder what would happen if God were to set up shop in a metro station?

I know what happened in the ME-free world of the garden. The grandness of God moved among his creation. The Bible states that God was "walking in the garden in the cool of the day."[2] We get the impression that this was, in biblical language, the time of day God would meet up with his creation—especially Adam and Eve—and spend time with them.

Nice picture isn't it? And I think it is safe to bet—not that I would bet since I am a pastor—but it is safe to *imagine* that God did spend perfect times of fellowship with the man and woman. Who knows what they talked about as they strolled together? God had given man the assignment of working the land and keeping it. Literally he was to *serve* the land and *protect* it. So maybe they talked about how to do that, and each morning God walked with them and gave them some direction for their day.

About the only other thing they were told to do was eat. You know that command: "eat of every tree of the garden, but of the tree of the knowledge of good and evil you shall not eat . . ."[3] On their daily strolls, they probably talked about lunch and what they were going to eat and what they had tried at the last tree. God was interested in them as companions.

So when God appears in Genesis 3:8, walking together was most likely a habit he and the humans had already developed. Humor me for a moment: raise your hand if you would—given the chance—spend that kind of time, "walking with God in the cool of the day"? (I can see imaginary hands going up all over the place.)

But like Joshua Bell in the metro station, most of us rush right past God daily, don't we? That's what our relationship with him is like in the ME-addicted world we live in. There are too many other things that get our attention: we have jobs to get to, work to do. We have Facebook to update, video games to play, other people to meet, chores to get done, books to read and movies to watch.

All Adam and Eve had was fruit, and apparently a lot of fruit. Yet only one was a "delight to the eyes."[4] Eve's eyes moved off of God and to the fruit. From that point on, the daily walks with God changed.

Instead of going on a walk with God, Adam and Eve went into hiding from God. Their reaction reveals two things:

- Humans were made to have intimate daily walks with God.
- At one time they were so intimate with God they immediately felt guilt and shame when they sinned.

Maybe this is why we have difficulty spending time with God. We do, don't we? Let's be honest. Even as a preacher, it is much easier for me to talk *about* God, study *about* God, write sermons and lessons and articles *about* God . . . than it is to merely *spend* time *with* God. We find distractions that keep us *away* from God: Twitter, Facebook, music, iPhones, iPods, iPads. It's the crisis of an "iFaith" generation. Our focus shifted from God to "me."

Why do we fill our time with distractions? Because a walk in the ME-addicted world with God is not so much a walk in paradise. At times he comes with correction. He may love us, but he does not love sin. So God cannot walk with us and ignore the "elephant in the room" (or maybe that is "garden"). He will expose what Jeremiah called a "desperately wicked heart."[5]

And so we follow Adam and Eve into hiding. We hide in our routines. We hide in our jobs. We hide in our friendships. We hide in our music and our games and our vacations and our constant going.

How is that working for us? If we are honest, not very well. We are more overscheduled, overdrawn, overworked, overfed, and over worried than ever before. Just perform your own social experiment. Watch people as they walk into your workplace or school or board meeting. What do you see? Most likely you see the walking dead. They look like they are in a major coma or have a hangover or are just dead tired.

That's the outcome when we follow Adam and Eve into hiding. But you know we don't have to follow them. We can follow Jesus instead. And when we do, we find someone who is unhurried; unstressed; had enough for each day, and more importantly, someone who spent time with God in the cool of the day.

The book of Mark tells us that Jesus got up "early in the morning, while it was still dark . . . departed and went out to a desolate place, and there he prayed."[6] If you read the entire context, he was as busy as us: teaching demands, people pressing in, needs to be met. But he still got away for a walk with God.

And because he did, we can too. We can walk with God. Mark Galli writes these insightful words:

> But that doesn't mean entertaining the Holy Presence is pain-free. Before the healing of forgiveness comes, there is the pain of God's probing deeply into our souls and discovering the ugliness of diseases that fester there. It includes a redemptive suffering as God cleanses the tender wounds opened by his love.[7]

God will probe into our souls and our lives, and this is what we are afraid of. We are afraid he'll find out what we are like and what we have done, and he won't "get" us and will just be mad at us.

But he does get us. The writer of the book of Hebrews reminds us: "For we do not have a high priest who is unable to sympathize with our weaknesses, but one who in every respect has been tempted as we are, yet without sin. Let us then with confidence draw near to the throne of grace, that we may receive mercy and find grace to help in time of need."[8]

So let me ask again: do you really want to walk with God in the cool of the day? If so, here are some interesting benefits.

Andrew Newberg, M.D., a pioneer in the field of neurotheology, wrote a book called *How God Changes Your Brain*. In it he states that twenty minutes of daily meditation can alter the brain structurally and therefore functionally. He says that changes in key areas allow us to be more compassionate and empathetic and allow us to handle stress a little better.[9]

People in biblical times understood the art of meditation. They practiced it.[10] That's why the Bible doesn't have any lengthy "Meditation 101" section in it. They did not have bibles, so they listened well and meditated on Scripture and hid it in their hearts. Paul wrote these words in Romans 12:2: "Do not be conformed to this world, but be transformed by the renewal of your mind . . ."

And how does that happen? We meditate and ponder and think about the things of God. A renewed mind leads to a new life. New thoughts lead to new behavior by "presenting our bodies as a living sacrifice . . . to God."[11] If we give God our time, he gets us. He changes us. We become more like him. We won't ever be in perfect unity with him this side of heaven, but we can become more closely so.

But the question is, "Do we give him any time?" It's interesting to me that we pass by God in our daily lives just as the people passed by Bell in the metro. We come to churches all across America and we suddenly give attention to the music, the volume, the message, but not necessarily to be with God. More often than not, we give our attention to the critique of these things.

It's our culture. One of my professors in college liked to say that if we did not worship God during the week, we would come to a corporate time of worship and it would be like the dry heaves: you try to bring up something but it's just not there. We don't know how to worship, so instead we complain.

Jerry Allen, a friend who recently returned from eighteen months of work in Qatar, was a part of a church there. I asked him if the church ever complained about the things we complain about: song selection, music volume, type of coffee. He said simply, with a slight smile, "No."

That culture will never change unless we change. And we will not change if we are ME-addicted. Only when we sit in the presence of God will we change. It is there we find that we have enough. We create a time in the day where God can sift through our soul, clean out the mess, and be with us.

How do you do this? Do as Jesus did. Get up. Get away. Be still. Be quiet. These are not easy things for us. Our ME-addicted world has trained us to stay busy and stay noisy so that we do not have to notice God. We have to retrain our ways by renewing our minds.

Schedule time with God just as you would any other appointment. Get away from the TV and technology. You may just find silence. I doubt God and the first humans kept up a constant chatter; His presence for them would have been enough.

You may want to go for an actual walk with God. Find a garden or a park. Strangely enough, walking thirty minutes a few times a week does wonders for the body:

- It helps you reduce your weight.
- It lowers high blood pressure.
- It lowers the risk of heart disease, stroke, and diabetes.
- It reduces anxiety and depression, boosting your mood.
- It helps you handle stress.
- It helps you feel more energetic and helps you sleep better.
- It improves your self-esteem

Just imagine what a walk with God will do for you.

Calvin Myint walked past the violinist in the metro station, got to the top of the escalator and went out a door to the street. Just a few hours later he had no memory that there had been a musician anywhere in sight.

"Where was he, in relation to me?"

"About four feet away."

"Oh."

There's nothing wrong with Myint's hearing. He had buds in his ear. He was listening to his iPod. There was nothing inherently wrong with what he was doing. He just missed an amazing opportunity.

Don't miss yours. God is near. He's walking in the garden in the cool of the day. You were made to walk with him. Will you be distracted or will you join him?

Chapter 3

A World with Boundaries

We understand when a parent says, "Do not run into the street!"

We "get it" when a waitress says, "Do not touch. The plate is extremely hot."

We have no issues when we're told, "Do not drink that—it's poison!"

But we have a lifetime of questions when God says, "Do not—" When he says "do not," we:

- Do not—think about the safety he is supplying.
- Do not—think about the protection he is presenting.
- Do not—think about the care he is conferring.

Our reaction is as old as Adam and Eve. God had created everything they needed for a fulfilling life in the garden. Lights? Check. Water? Check. Land? Check. Plants?. Animals? Check. Check. Partner for life? Check.

Oh, and perfect union with God? Very checked.

Before God placed mankind on this earth, he placed everything they would need on this earth. He first prepared a place for them. Like a master builder he had a plan for how this would happen, but unlike builders we know, God did not need a tool belt. He needed only his voice. God would say, "Let there be—" whatever he wanted to create. Immediately following, the Scriptures say, "And it was so."

It was the perfect picture of paradise. Like an all-inclusive resort, everything they could possibly want was at their fingertips. The woman never had to worry about the man leaving his dirty clothes lying around. There was an endless buffet of food for all that no one had to cook. Provision was made for all the day-to-day needs.

We like resorts. In our day, resorts are where we go to get away from work and troubles. But in this ME-free world of the garden, there was even more that God had put in place for the man and woman. He did not just plop them down in this little paradise and allow them to laze around all day. Aside from the garden, there were three more things in his creation design that they needed.

God gave them a vocation. Notice that is *vocation* and not *vacation.* In the ME-free world a vacation was not necessary, but a vocation was. The humans needed something to do to contribute to the world God had created. In the same way that God tends and cares for us, he wants us to share in the same vocation. Work was part of creation in the ME-free world. And apparently the humans had no reason to vacate from it.

And so we read, "The Lord God took the man and put him in the garden of Eden to work it and keep it."[1] The word pair *work* and *keep* can also be translated as *serve* and *protect* or *till* and *keep.* The words suggest either gardening or shepherding. In either case, work belongs in the ME-free world. And it is work that is meant to enhance the garden, not spoil it. Man was given a vocation where God entrusted him with this garden to share in God's work.

God gave them permission. Settle into your first experience of an all-inclusive resort and one of the first questions you might have is, "Can we just get food off the buffet at any time? Can we just walk up and get a drink whenever we want?" Imagine having the world at your fingertips! So God says to his humans, "You may surely eat of every tree of the garden . . ."[2]

This freedom is for the good of mankind. It is for his sustenance. It is so he can live in the way God intends for him to live. The

Corinthian church had it right in essence when they said, "All things are lawful for me . . ."[3] Paul quotes what they were saying and does not refute their ideas outright.

God also gave them a prohibition. God adds a corrective to Adam and Eve. And Paul adds a corrective when he says, "but not all things are helpful" and, "but I will not be enslaved by anything."[4] Some things can hurt us. Too much of some things can take us over. Paul understood the importance of this third thing. God said to Adam and Eve, "but of the tree of the knowledge of good and evil you shall not eat . . ."[5]

As soon as we read these words we react in exactly the same way Adam and Eve did once the serpent found them. We want to know "why not?" We want to know "why would God do this?" And, destructively, we want to go and find out what that fruit is all about.

There's not much in the story to help us with our ME-centered questions. Nothing is explained. There is nothing about the tree. We don't even get to know what kind of fruit it was. (Was it really an apple?) We don't get everything we'd like answered in the Bible or by this God. But we can make some observations.

One observation is something about us. In addition to this perfect plan and place of a paradise that God created for his people, he gave them three things: a vocation, permission and a prohibition. *One* prohibition. Out of all the work they could do and out of all the fruit they had permission to enjoy, the *one* thing they and we focus on is the *one* prohibition.

The other observation is something about God, and it is this: he is God. And the most foundational thing in this episode of our story is that God has the authority to command something and the expectation is that we will obey.

But that probably does not satisfy us any more than having plenty of work to do and plenty of fruit to eat satisfied Adam and Eve. So let's look at this some more. The big question that comes up is "If God knew the humans would sin, then why did he set them up for a fall?" I think the question is wrong. God did not set them up for a fall. Satan gets credit for that. God set them up to become the kind of humans he created them to be.

Some call this choice in the garden *free will*. It's not a bad concept. It helps us to understand that God has arranged our world in a way that we can grow and develop into good people. How does that happen? It happens now like it did then. We become good people when we make choices that glorify God.

We can understand this when we look at parents and their children. At some point parents have to allow their children to begin making their own choices. If a parent does this too soon, like when their child is five years old, we think they are not practicing good parenting principles. But likewise, when they are still controlling their child at twenty-five years of age, we sense something is desperately wrong and dysfunctional.

So there is a time when we cannot and should not control them. And it's tough on parents. We don't know all we'd like to know. We don't know all the places they are going and the choices they are making. But we have to cut loose the apron strings to allow them to become people who make choices and have a good character and glorify God with their lives.

God does the same with his children, even in the garden. Maybe you think you would not have set it up this way. And if you think that, then you are showing a symptom of the ME-addiction—and, I might add, you are very inconsistent. Here's what people do: They want "freedom" from a God who has set up some prohibitions, or boundaries for our good. We accept the lie that God is trying to prevent us from having some fun. Just like Adam and Eve, we think there is something we are missing so we go after it.

And when we do, our lives blow up in our faces. Our souls become stained. Our world deteriorates. When it does, we immediately begin to ask why this God did not make the world in such a way that we did not have a choice. It's an endless cycle because we do not understand nor accept what it is God is after.

The issue in the garden is not so much free will as it is character. God wants your character and mine to form in a good way. Our world needs people with good character. They stand out in the crowd. We say there is *something* about them. They are like light in the darkness. They season the groups they are a part of like salt seasons food.

And so God sets the world up in such a way that our characters can form. The problem is that our characters can go wrong. We seem to like to push the boundaries of what is good for us.

When our first son, Kris, was two years old, he was very strong willed. He had done some defiant act that warranted a time-out. We put him in his room and told him that we wanted him to stay there. We even pointed to a line that separated his room from the hallway and said, "Do not let your foot cross that line. For in the day your foot crosses that line you will surely die." (Okay, we didn't really say that last line, but we did look sternly at him.)

A few minutes later we peered down the hallway and saw one little toe crossing the line. We had to laugh, too. But don't we do the same? Don't we test the boundaries we are given? A teenager gets a curfew of midnight and rolls in at 12:10 a.m. A boss asks an employee to arrive for work at 8:30 a.m., and the employee drags in at 8:39 a.m. The curfew is there for safety. The starting time is there to help create a productive work environment. There are boundaries for our good, but we push them. When we do, there are usually some consequences that follow.

When you push God's boundaries for you, there will be consequences, too, but he will not stop you. God is not a party crasher. People don't like party crashers. Tareq and Michaele Salahi discovered that truth when they allegedly crashed a White House state dinner on November 24, 2009. It caused quite a media storm.[6] Good people do not crash parties or intrude where they are not welcome.

God is good. He does not go where he is not invited. So God gives us space. He gives us choices and he allows us to answer the question that we most need to answer. This particular story about creation and us and our world leads us not to the questions of "why?" and "Did God set us up for a fall?" The big question of the garden is: "Would you like there to be a God?"[7] The question is not "Do you believe in a God?" The question is: "Would you like there to be a God?"

The real story that is going on in Genesis 3 is about whether or not you or I want there to be a God. Because if you do want a God then you will have to give up your ME-addiction. You have to decide that you will not be God but instead let God be God. God's kingdom overrides yours and mine. We will find ourselves back in the garden with the choice of trusting God and seeing our character develop in a good way. Or will we trust our own judgment, push God aside, and push his boundaries to our own detriment?

Our ME-addiction causes us to doubt God when he says "do not." We think his boundaries are keeping us out of something good, as if he had some inside track on the latest fun and doesn't want to share it. Heard through the ME-addiction, "do not" causes us to disobey God and follow another path. When we choose another path, we sin.

But there is another choice that can be made. It is the choice to trust and obey. With the simplicity of a trusting child, when our Father says "do not," we simply "do not." We do the work he has given us to do. We enjoy the multitude of things he has given us to enjoy.

Don't you want there to be a God like that, one that gives you worth and work, and one that gives you over-the-top blessings? There is a God like that. And you can find him if you seek him.[8]

Chapter 4

Created for Community

It's a picture of what you most want. It's a picture of what you most need. And I have a snapshot of it right here for you today. Don't get too excited—it isn't the latest smart phone or tablet. But it does have to do with connectivity.

The picture is found in Genesis 1:27:

> So God created man in his own image,
> in the image of God he created him;
> male and female he created them.

It is quite something to know we are made in the image of God. But what does that mean?

For starters, how we "look" on the outside has nothing to do with this image. The word means *likeness* or literally a *shadowing forth*. It isn't God, but it has the same likeness of God—kind of like your shadow cast on a sunny day: It is close to you, it has the same shape as you., but it isn't you.

You may notice in your Bible that this verse is laid out in poetic form. The third line explains the first two. How did God create mankind in his image? He created them male and female.

Some take this to mean that you can't really get an idea of the image of God unless you see a couple. Some couples, working together to live out the "God image," do well. Still other couples are far from displaying the image of God. And Jesus—a single person—was said to be the "image of the invisible God"[1] and the "exact imprint of his nature."[2]

So we know that although a man and woman can reflect the image of God together, this is not what the passage means. The two New Testament claims about Jesus can help us understand what the shadowing forth of God is about. The word for *image* has to do with "one in whom the likeness of any one is seen." We get our word *icon* from the Greek word that is used here. The phrase *exact imprint* comes from a Greek word which we transliterate *character*. This image, then, has more to do with how we are seen in our *behavior*.

Whenever you and I demonstrate the character of God and whenever his likeness can be seen in us, then we most live into in his image. And that likeness is best seen in relationship. God says, "Let *us* make man in *our* image . . ." This is the one God in three persons speaking. If we can picture how God relates within the Godhead, we will have a picture of our image.

John of Damascus, an eighth-century Christian monk, described the relationship of the Godhead as perichoresis, which means a "circle dance." He said it was a "cleaving together," that the Father, Son and Spirit "not only embrace each other, but they also enter into each other, permeate each other, and dwell in each other. One in being, they are also always one in the intimacy of their friendship."[3]

What John is saying is that the Godhead likes each other. Even loves each other. Can you imagine the Father walking in and finding the Son and the Spirit arguing with each other? Can you see the Son walking into the room and the Father and Spirit snubbing him? Of course not!

And in the ME-free world of the garden you cannot imagine Adam and Eve not getting along either. They loved each other perfectly. They loved God perfectly. As we have seen, they "walked together in the cool of the day." When Eve walked on the scene, Adam did not feel threatened. He did not think God would love her any more than God loved him—in fact, he sang a song about her.[4] You could say they were a match made in heaven.

They did not sit down in the garden, one behind the other, the one behind the other looking at the back of the other's head, as if they were sitting in a theater full of people they did not know, like we do at concerts or at church. They did not complain about anything; instead, they looked out for each other and cared for each other. Just like the Godhead did. They lived out the image of God.

But something changed, didn't it? The ME-addiction hit both of them and relationships have never been the same. You can tell just by going to church. You'd think that would be the place people would always behave as if they are made in the image of God. But it isn't always so.

For instance, have there been times you walked into a church gathering without thinking about anyone but yourself or anything but your own problems? Have there been times you went through the motions of worship without considering how you could build someone else up or encourage them? Have there been times you attended a worship gathering looking mainly for what it would do for you, asking, "What's in it for ME?" Most likely we all have on occasion.

Here's another question: Have you ever had times where you would much rather cocoon yourself from people instead of engaging people? How difficult is it to spend any amount of time with anyone else, either from your church or social networks? Have you ever thought, "No one ever invites me to lunch or over to their house"? That may be true. But who said it was up to someone else to make the first move toward relationship?

The way we operate in our lives and in our churches gives us a hint that there is something amiss. It shows that something changed from the garden. The ME-addiction has spread to all of us.

I'm a minister and I love the people at my church. But honestly, some mornings I do not want to be there. And it's not so I can just spend time with God. It's just because I'd rather be alone. Sometimes I feel like Barry.

One Sunday morning, Barry woke up to his wife shaking him by the shoulder. "You have to get up," she said. "We have to get ready for church."

"I don't want to go to church," he replied. "I want to stay in bed."

Not happy with his response his wife insisted, "Give me three good reasons why you should stay in bed and not go to church."

"OK," he answered. "First, I don't get anything out of the service. Second, I don't like the people there. And third, no one there likes me. Now can you give me three good reasons why I should go to church?"

His wife responded, "First, it will do you some good. Second, there are people who really do like you and they'll miss you if you aren't there. And third, you're the minister!"

But God says, "It is not good for the man to be alone."[5] Why? Because we are made in the image of God and God is a God of relationship. He made us for relationship.

Another indication there is something wrong is found throughout the New Testament. The church, or the body of Christ, has to be reminded and taught that they are to love one another. You'd think it would be automatic for people who were made in the image of God to love one another. But we don't naturally do that.

So Jesus tells his followers: "A new commandment I give to you, that you love one another: just as I have loved you, you also are to love one another. By this all people will know that you are my disciples, if you have love for one another."[6]

The old commandment was to love your neighbor as you love yourself. One could use the old commandment as a rationale for living a ME-centered life. The rationale could go something like this: Some days I don't love myself too much, so I don't have to love my neighbor too much. I don't want to talk to myself, so I don't talk to my neighbor. I don't want to be bothered, so I don't bother my neighbor. I'm too lazy to mow my own lawn so I definitely will not go to the trouble of mowing his.

But to love as Jesus loved? That's a whole different story. If we love as Jesus did, ME disappears. Jesus loved us by putting our needs ahead of his. ME recedes to the background while HE becomes the focus. When he does, our character changes and we live in ways that demonstrate the image of God.

Loving that way is not easy. Instead, we'd prefer a lesson on love. We want to know the four Greek words for love, which one is used most in the New Testament, and what Jesus meant by "agape." And then we move on to another lesson—something less personal like the allegorical meaning of Balaam's donkey or the etymology of the word millennium. Those things keep our mind on other very important and deep things so we don't have to love.

Juan Carlos Ortiz tells of how he decided to teach his church this verse one Sunday morning:[7] He got up to preach and said, "The message for today is 'Love One Another'" and then he sat down. Everyone just sat there, waiting for what would happen next. So Ortiz got up again and said, "The message for today is 'Love One Another'" and then again sat down. The third time he went to the pulpit he said, "The message for today is, 'Love One Another,' and until we begin doing that, there won't be any more messages."

The New Testament does the same thing. It hits this subject over and over again from different angles. Here are a few examples:

- "Love one another with brotherly affection."[8] The words here describe the mutual love of siblings in a family should have for each other. They aren't talking about a mushy feeling as much as referring to the fact that in a real family each member has the other person's back.
- "Rejoice with those who rejoice; weep with those who weep."[9] Hard to do this if we don't know much about each other, isn't it?—and it takes time, something we are sometimes unwilling to give.
- "Therefore welcome one another as Christ has welcomed you, for the glory of God."[10] Christ accepted you with all your issues and he says we should do that with each other. To *accept* means to *take someone's hand*, to *be a companion*, or to *give someone access to your heart*.

- "Greet one another with a holy kiss."[11] Depending on who you are sitting by, this may be a good one. Notice this is found in Romans. Italians know how to greet each other. They grab you and plant a solid kiss on each cheek. Now, this doesn't mean we have to go around kissing each other on both cheeks. But it does speak to a form of greeting someone more warmly than someone you don't know. There is a relationship involved.

- "All of you agree, and that there be no divisions among you, but that you be united in the same mind and the same judgment."[12] We have to know that we are on each other's side and will take up for each other. If you belong to a church long enough, you will find there will be people from time to time who get upset or think they know what is best, and they will try to divide the church. But we need to agree on what we are about and what we value so that we can just show those people the door. God loves unity. And we should too.

- "Bearing with one another and, if one has a complaint against another, forgiving each other; as the Lord has forgiven you, so you also must forgive."[13] I am a sinful person. Come to think of it, we all are, so put two of us in the same room and at times we will not get along. We will do and say things that will hurt each other. Not necessarily intentionally. But in those times we have to put up with each other and forgive. Paul adds, "as the Lord forgave you." In other words, if Jesus forgave you, how can you not forgive each other? Stop keeping a record against everyone. Move on. Grow up!

- "Addressing one another in psalms and hymns and spiritual songs, singing and making melody to the Lord with your heart . . ."[14] A good place to start would be to speak to each other. And one way the church has done this is through the songs. We share our praises of God with each other.

- They would "teach and admonish" each other.[15] It is not just my job or the elders' job to teach or to admonish. If you see someone behaving in a way that does not "shadow forth" the image of God, it is your duty to talk to them. But do it in love.

- One last example. "not neglecting to meet together, as is the habit of some, but encouraging one another . . ."[16] Some say "I don't need the church. I can just do this God thing on my own." That's not biblical. But today we are ME-addicted and so we want to do Christianity on our own, even though the one we say we follow did not do it on his own. And why do we meet? Not just for the worship or teaching. Those are important. But just as important is the encouraging of each other. So when you meet, meet with the intention that you will find a way to encourage someone else.

There are many more of these "one another" verses in the Bible. They are not suggestions for God's people. They are commandments of how we are to relate to each other. And each of them shows us how to live in harmony as the Godhead lives in harmony.

How do we get there? First, you have to make time for other people. We say we don't have time, but we need to be truthful. We have just as much time as Jesus did—twenty-four hours in a day. The problem is our time is tied up in ME and MY things.

But when you love others you will have time for them. The young man who thinks his schedule is too full for anyone else and has no free nights suddenly finds time, when he meets the girl of his dreams, to spend four nights a week with her. How does he do it? He doesn't know. Love caused him to make the time.

The truth is we don't really love each other, do we? Not as Jesus loved us. Before you make time for people, then, you and I need to first love them. How can that happen when we are ME-addicted?

One remedy is to begin praying for people. Prayer is what Adam and Eve had in the garden in their walks with God. It is taking another person with us into the presence of God. If I pray for you, a love for you will grow and develop in me.

Then begin praying for yourself to have a love for people. We need to ask God to give us a hunger to be like him. I like the story of Teresa of Avila. She was a Carmelite nun of the sixteenth century. She asked God to make her spend four hours a day in prayer with him. The answer she got from God was this: "Teresa, I don't make the little birds eat. When the little birds get hungry, they eat. And when you're hungry for me, you will spend more time with me . . ."[17]

In the same way, when we have a hunger to love as Jesus loved, we will spend time with each other, too.

After Ortiz said "Love one another" and sat down for the third time, a stirring moved through the church. People began talking to each other and asking if anyone knew what the preacher meant. Finally an elder stood up and, pointing to the person in the pew behind him, said, "I think I understand what Pastor Ortiz means. He wants me to love you. But how can I love you when I do not know you?"

He proceeded to introduce himself and began to meet others around him. Then others began doing the same; phone numbers were exchanged and. dinner invitations offered. Help was given where needed.

With just three simple words Ortiz had given his most powerful message. And his church began imaging God.

When you and I begin to shadow forth the image of God, there will be connectivity unlike any social network you can find.

It will be what you most want.

It will be what you most need.

Chapter 5

The Birth of the ME Addiction

If you've ever gone to a carnival, you've heard the voice. One minute you are walking around the carnival grounds taking in the sights of the Ferris wheel and the Tilt-a-Whirl and the mini roller coaster, wondering how secure the bolts and cables are before getting in line, plopping down a few tickets, and asking for your body to be jostled around like the inside of a washing machine. You're breathing in the smells of the funnel cakes and corn dogs, questioning to yourself whether these stands are ever inspected for health code standards.

You're thinking, "Life is good"—until inadvertently you turn down the *midway*.

The next minute you are suddenly surrounded by a dizzying array of games. Basketball hoops so small in design and basketballs so overinflated that even Kobe couldn't make a basket. Milk bottles stacked in a way that Roy Oswalt wouldn't be able to knock them down. Skee Ball games that the best bowler in the world couldn't defeat. (I would have inserted a name here but have no idea who the top bowler is.)

You know you should just keep walking. But then you hear the voice. The carnival "barker" begins yipping at your heels. "Your lady needs a prize. Are you man enough to win one for her?" You know that winning a stuffed animal does not prove your manhood. Hunting wild boar with your bare hands might, but not this.

You start to move on. But then it comes again. "See that guy? He just won a top-shelf prize for his girl." You look over to see a giant stuffed giraffe. It's moving! Then you realize a junior high school boy, all of 5 feet 2 inches tall, is carrying this monstrosity off with his Miley Cyrus wannabe girlfriend who looks like she has landed the man of her dreams at thirteen years old.

The barker has supplied the stimulus. He is waiting for your response—and in the gap is your choice.

The carnival barker has been around since the beginning. One day Eve was walking through the carnival grounds we know as the garden of Eden. The sights were spectacular. The smells were unspoiled.

Life was good. We know that because of the last verse in Genesis 2. "And the man and his wife were both naked and were not ashamed."[1] That's the equivalent of the nice stroll through the carnival grounds enjoying the sights and smells. Kind of.

But then we turn the page to Genesis 3 and we find ourselves on the midway. There's no explanation of where the serpent came from or how he got there. That's not the point. The point is, he is there. He is the voice of the carnival barker. And he provides the stimulus.

> Now the serpent was more crafty than any other
> beast of the field that the Lord God had made. He said
> to the woman, "Did God actually say, 'You shall not eat
> of any tree in the garden'?"[2]

Before the voice, the woman was moving along just fine. After the voice, she paused. Carnival barkers know how to push your buttons. So did the serpent. We are told the serpent was "crafty." In Scripture, the word for *crafty* carries the idea of "wisdom" and a "nimble and skillful ability." It is a neutral term and can be positive or negative.

In case you're wondering, here it is negative. The serpent is intent on pulling the woman away from her planned path. Notice how he does it. He makes her question God with a slight twist. "Did God really say, 'You must not eat from any tree in the garden'?"

The serpent confused the woman. And in case you are confused, go back and reread what God had said. "You may surely eat of every tree of the garden, but of the tree of the knowledge of good and evil you shall not eat, for in the day that you eat of it you shall surely die."[3]

How quickly we forget. The woman answers the serpent by saying, "We may eat of the fruit of the trees in the garden, but God said, 'You shall not eat of the fruit of the tree that is in the midst of the garden, neither shall you touch it, lest you die.'"[4]

She makes about one of the three basketball throws. She knocks down the top milk bottle but leaves the others standing. God had told Adam and Eve they could eat fruit from the trees in the garden and that they must not eat from the tree of the knowledge of good and evil, but he did not say they could not *touch* it.

Eve is in the moment of choice, and in that moment she is choosing poorly. She has forgotten God's word. And then the serpent lies outright in a crafty way. "You will not surely die," the serpent said to the woman. "You will not surely die. For God knows that when you eat of it your eyes will be opened, and you will be like God, knowing good and evil."[5] After they ate of the fruit, they did know good and evil. Before they did not know good *and* evil, only good. In that sense they were now like God. But they are unlike God in that they do not know how to handle evil. God understands it, hates it, but has no part in it. From this point on, Adam and Eve will have trouble staying away from it.

And what about not dying? The moment after the first crunch of the fruit you would think they would have dropped dead on the ground. But they didn't, did they? Adam lived to be 930 years old.[6] There's no clue as to how old he was when he bit into the fruit. My guess is he was about 465 years old and this was the first case of mid-life crisis. Regardless, he must have lived a few hundred years after it, albeit with maybe a bad case of indigestion. So who's telling the truth?

Death can mean more than physical death. Like the barker who does not tell his unsuspecting victim that his chances of leaving disappointed and with less cash are very high, the serpent did not paint Adam and Eve an entire picture. He did not tell them that they would immediately feel shame. He did not tell them they would now feel as if they had to hide from God. He did not tell them that one of their sons would kill the other.

But unlike the barker who lets his victim leave with the same feelings of disappointment, shame, and resentment, God does something different. It may be that the word *die* is to be taken literally. It has to do with a *violent* death. But instead of allowing that to happen, God begins to put his mercy into motion. The first sacrifice for sin is given—he made clothes out of animal skins to cover the humans. Imagine the *violence* of that scene. Much later, Christ will die a *violent* death on a cross in God's greatest act of grace.

And although he sends them out of the garden, as much for their own protection as for punishment, he still has a relationship with them as he helps mankind deal with this newfound ME-addiction that causes them to choose their way over God's way.

Call it an addiction or call it sin, but "it" permeates our being. In the New Testament, Paul speaks of this addiction when he speaks of "the law of sin that dwells in my members."[7] An addiction is something that has become a habit. At one time it was not a habit.

At one time you did not listen to the barker—but then you did, just once. And ever since then you have been trying to win the prize.

At one time you did not drink alcohol—then it became a habit out of control, and it was hard to stop.

At one time you did not gossip—but then you listened for the first time. Next you shared something you knew you should not have. But you liked the feeling of power you gained from having some knowledge to share—and it did not stop.

In each case you were tempted (the stimulus) to do or say something. You had time to choose, and then you responded. After awhile these "sins" become ingrained, not only in our psyche but also in our "members," or our bodies. They become the way we are.

Satan knows that. In C.S. Lewis's *Screwtape Letters*, Screwtape is working with his young apprentice demon named Wormwood. Wormwood is getting a reprimand for allowing his target to become a Christian. But Screwtape says, "There is no need to despair; hundreds of these adult converts have been reclaimed after a brief sojourn in the enemy's camp and are now with us. All habits of the patient, both mental and bodily, are still in our favour."[8]

Satan knows that most followers of Christ do not follow Christ. If they did, their habits would change. They merely want their ticket to heaven but do not want to live as if they are in heaven now. He knows that more people are merely good church members—people who show up some Sundays and put some money in the plate and go on their own way by Monday—rather than disciples—people who follow Jesus every day and whose lives are informed by his life.

And so the sin habits remain. Adam and Eve knew a time without these sin habits. We have not. Paul makes it clear that everyone since Adam, with the exception of Jesus, has sinned.[9] We come to God with these habits intact. For us to change, our habits must change. We need to hear another voice that has more power than that of the carnival barker.

That voice is the voice of Jesus,. and that voice must be heard in the space between the stimulus (i.e. temptation) and the response called choice. Old habits have to be broken. New habits must be made. How can that happen?

It begins by getting a clear picture of who you are in Christ. Paul calls this *reckoning*. It is knowing that you want more than anything else to be like Christ. And if you have been identified with Christ through baptism, he says that you "must consider yourselves dead to sin and alive to God in Christ Jesus."[10] *Consider* is sometimes translated *reckon* as in:

"Are you going to lunch?"

"I reckon so."

It means to *take into account* or *deliberate*.

Your identity strongly influences your actions. The more secure I am in my manhood, the less frequently some annoying barker who blitzes through town will be able to push my buttons and cajole me into wasting my money on his unwinnable game. And the more secure you are in Christ, the less frequently the serpent will be able to talk you into something that is not who you are.

How do you get this vision? By spending a lot of time with Jesus. Read the gospels, get to know his words, watch what he does, follow him where he goes, and most importantly, turn your heart toward him. The important question here is, *"Do you want to be with Jesus?"* If your answer is yes, you will follow him wherever he goes so you can be with him wherever he is.

And that leads to the next practice that will change your habits from bad ones to good ones. If you want to be with Jesus, then you will do the things Jesus did. Jesus did things that allowed him, when faced with a choice, to press the pause button before he responded.

When our boys were little, we learned that when we walked through certain sections of the store we would be bombarded with stimuli. "You are the best dad in the world if you buy me that Dragonzord." "You are the best mom in the world if you buy me Count Chocula." The temptation was strong. We wanted to be the best mom and dad in the world. But we quickly learned we were going to be the most broke mom and dad in the world if we kept responding to their stimuli.

So we learned to say, "Okay. Let's wait one week and then we can get it." We pushed the pause button. And a week from then they did not even remember what it was they wanted.

In the same way, God has given us ways to create new habits in our members. Paul refers to this when he writes, "Do not present your members to sin as instruments for unrighteousness, but present yourselves to God as those who have been brought from death to life, and your members to God as instruments for righteousness."[11]

We tend to think that the sin in us is only in our minds. But according to Paul, sin is also in our bodies. And that makes sense, doesn't it? You can sin just in your mind by thinking bad things, but sin most often comes out through our mouth or our actions. Our bodies are part of it.

And so we have to retrain our bodies. They have become couch potatoes, lethargic and lazy in the battle against sin. So Paul uses an athletic term and tells us to "train yourself for godliness."[12] The word *train* means "to exercise vigorously, in any way, either the body or the mind."

Paul did this, and so did Jesus. Their training consisted of moving their minds and bodies into exercises like solitude, fasting, prayer, private study, communal study, worship, sacrificial service, and giving. Each of these practices pushes the pause button and allows us to choose wisely before responding.

Dallas Willard remarks that "Solitude is the most radical of the disciplines for life in the spirit."[13] Just getting away from all the other voices so that you can hear God's voice is the number one exercise in your training regimen.

Breaking the ME-addiction is not easy. The habits have been ingrained since the beginning of time. You have listened to the barker. You have wasted time. You have made poor decisions and created bad habits.

But you can change. God did not leave Adam and Eve alone and he has not left you alone either. He has given you his son, Jesus Christ, who you can follow into a new life. He will surface the stimuli that tempts you so that you can see it. He does this not for your condemnation but for your transformation. He will help you change your habitual responses.

That change can really happen in your life. The question is, "Do you want to be like Jesus more than anything else in this world?" He has given you a training path to follow.

But you still might want to avoid the carnival midway.

Chapter 6

A ME-Sized Appetite

I don't know who decided that churches should meet in mid-to-late morning—just long enough past breakfast but close enough to lunch. It's tough on preachers, because by the time we are doing our best to turn people's attention to a message from God, stomachs are doing their best to turn people's attention to food. My gut feeling is, more often than not, that the stomach wins the battle.

"Hey, getting a little hungry down here. You gonna do something about it?!"

Next thing you know your mind has taken a seat at the same table as your stomach. You picture a plate of pasta or a pan of pizza and before long you're longing for food. You miss the second point of the sermon as you dream of a second serving of spaghetti.

It's a culinary shame that, unbeknownst to all but the most devoted disciple, you have more food right in front of you than meets the eye.

Eve might have been feeling a few hunger pangs herself when the serpent mentioned food. Like a growling stomach he pulled her attention to her midsection and away from God.

> Now the serpent was more crafty than any other beast
> of the field that the Lord God had made. He said to the

woman, "Did God actually say, 'You shall not eat of any
tree in the garden'?"[1]

Just like you are thinking about pasta and pizza now that I
mentioned it, Eve started thinking about eating. She had a whole
supermarket of fruit to pick and choose from. And that was all fine
until the serpent turned her senses to one tree and one fruit.

That's when she saw it. "So when the woman saw that the tree
was good for food, and that it was a delight to the eyes, and that
the tree was to be desired to make one wise, she took of its fruit
and ate."[2] Once she saw it, she had to have it. The word for *see* here
is not a word for a mere glance. It means that she looked *intently* at
it. She *gazed* upon it. She *learned* about it.

Was she mesmerized by it? Did she Google it to find the
calories it contained? I can't tell you what all that means. I can
tell you that as long as the fruit captivated her attention, God
did not, and that was the first step toward a ME-addiction. There
was enough food already. There was God, but now she wanted
something more. And as long as she picked fruit over God, she
would always be hungry.

It's not too hard to understand Eve. You've seen things too
that you then "took" and "ate." And you did it because you were
hungry: hungry for food, hungry for love, hungry for adventure.

The Bible calls this hunger *desire*. Jesus' closest disciple spoke of
this desire when he wrote this admonition: "Do not love the world
or the things in the world. If anyone loves the world, the love of
the Father is not in him. For all that is in the world—the desires
of the flesh and the desires of the eyes and pride in possessions—is
not from the Father but is from the world."[3]

In other versions, the idea of desire is translated as *cravings*.
Cravings is a word I can sink my teeth into. When we were in
Europe we were introduced to Nutella. Nutella is a spread made
of hazelnuts, almonds and a hint of chocolate. The first batch of
Nutella was sold in 1946. Later, the first jar to be distributed across
Europe was sent on April 20, 1964 (in honor of my birthday which
is April 20, 1960; a very nice gesture from the Ferrero family).

It didn't pass across my palette until our trip in 2008. We discovered chocolate crepes in Paris. The chocolate filling came from Nutella. The first bite brought pleasure to my taste buds. Before long I began to crave Nutella. So did Karen. Each morning in Paris she would get this crazed look in her eyes. She would begin pacing the floors of our rental, and I would go out in search of some Nutella laden pastry. I'd bring it back to her along with a jar of the stuff. She's take a hit—I mean a bite—and she would begin to calm again.

Sometimes we would eat just enough. But there were other times the Nutella would take over and we would finish and fight over who got to lick the remnants of the jar. Then we would wonder, "Why did we eat so much?" What was a pleasure became a problem.

And herein is found the dilemma of desires. We have them. God wired us with them. He even gave us a world in which to experience pleasure. Let me remind you that all desire is not sinful. The same word used in John's writing is used elsewhere of proper desires:

- "And he said to them," I have earnestly *desired* to eat this Passover with you before I suffer."[4]
- "I am hard pressed between the two. My *desire* is to depart and be with Christ, for that is far better. But to remain in the flesh is more necessary on your account."[5]
- "But since we were torn away from you, brothers, for a short time, in person not in heart, we endeavored the more eagerly and with great *desire* to see you face to face . . ."[6]

Jesus had a desire to share the Passover meal with his friends. Paul desired to go ahead and die and be with Christ. Paul also desired to be with those he had introduced to Christ. These are obviously good desires.

But in most instances in Scripture this word is used with a negative connotation. Listen to these words from the Apostle Paul:

- "But put on the Lord Jesus Christ, and make no provision for the flesh, to gratify its desires."[7]
- "But I say, walk by the Spirit, and you will not gratify the desires of the flesh."[8]

What are we to do with this? Is all desire and all things that bring pleasure "sinful"? You probably sense the answer is no. But some people have a view of Christianity that would argue that God is like the "parent in the sky," saying no to all the fun stuff there is to do.

Before our first son was born I started walking around the house, randomly saying, "no." One day Karen, concerned I was turning senile at a young age, asked, "Rick, why are you walking around saying 'no' all the time?"

I said, "Look, we are about to have a child. Before we know it, he will be a teenager. I figure it's never too early to start practicing."

Sometimes we think God operates the same way, which is a sad thing when you consider who it was that created food that delights the taste or who created the sights in nature that fills us with wonder or who created sex. God obviously wanted his creation to enjoy life.

That's why he gave Adam and Eve a garden full of pleasure. There was food everywhere, with one prohibition. There was pristine nature to explore. And can you imagine what Adam thought after spending who knows how long naming all the animals, suddenly falling asleep only to awake to the sight of Eve. All he had seen were buffaloes and baboons and giraffes and gazelles. Now he saw another human.

It was all good. Because at one time it was all enjoyed in relationship with God. God was the center of their lives. Anything they did was within his permission. And it was all pleasurable.

But once Eve's eyes left God and went after the fruit, things changed. Did the fruit still taste good? Sure, but the aftertaste was bitter. Did the world still offer adventure? More than they could experience, but it left them tired and aging. Was the sexual experience still pleasurable? You can bet on it. But the pages of the

Bible are filled with the disillusionments that crept in when the ME-addiction moved the focus of the act to self-satisfaction rather than mutual love.

Write down this recipe: anytime we move outside the boundaries that God has set for us, pleasure will become a problem. Take food, for instance. We were created with the need to refuel our bodies with calories that are burned for energy, and yet Western civilization has overdone its eating. We consume more food than most of the world. According to USDA research, Americans are consuming more food and hundreds more calories per day than a person from the 1950s.[9] The average food supply in 2000 was 3,800 calories per person per day. Of the 3,800 calories available to the average person, about 1,100 is lost to spoilage, plate waste, cooking and other wastes, making the our average caloric intake 2,700 calories. This is 800 more calories per person per day than someone from the 1950s. Data also suggests that we eat out more today and when we go out, we eat more or eat higher calorie foods, or both.

The study also goes on to show that sixty-two percent of American adults were overweight, up forty-six percent from 1980. Twenty-seven percent were so far overweight that they were classified as obese. We seem to have an obsession with food.

Jesus' disciples were obsessed with food in John 4. While he sat by Jacob's well, they went into town to find food. Jesus had a conversation with a woman about water and how the thirst she was experiencing in her soul could be satisfied by knowing him.

The disciples came back from their excursion into town. Jesus had been sitting at the well resting in the noonday heat. The most pressing thing to Jesus had been to care for the woman's soul. The most pressing thing to the disciples was food. So they urged him to eat. If this were you or me, we'd be ready to tear into a sack of Chic-Fil-A sandwiches. Not Jesus. He said, "I have food to eat that you do not know about."[10]

The disciples checked for camel tracks, thinking someone must have brought him something to eat while they were gone. So Jesus continued: "My food is to do the will of him who sent me and to accomplish his work."[11] His statement can help us curb our ME-sized appetite.

Jesus' goal was God. The disciples' goal was food. There's a big difference. Jesus restored the original state of the garden. He knew that God was the ultimate goal. God was the one who must captivate us.

Prior to their sin, Adam and Eve were captivated by God, and while they were, their God-given desires were satisfied. God-given desires will not make you less than what he wanted you to be, God-given desires will not divert you from a pursuit of the holy, and God-given desires will not move you off-track from what he has planned for your life.

It's when anything takes us away from God as our goal that we find ourselves unsatisfied and wanting more. Prior to their sin, Adam and Eve did not think there was something else they needed. After their sin, the fruit failed to satisfy. Instead of going back to what did satisfy, they began a never-ending search for something else.

Don't we do the same? We eat more than we need while much of the world goes malnourished. We spend a fortune on weekend trips, looking for something that we never find. And some, with a great love right in front of them, leave it, thinking there might be greener grass elsewhere.

The green grass you desire can be found. The cool water you thirst for is available. Jesus, the Good Shepherd, promises you water and bread.

> The Lord is my shepherd; I shall not want.
> He makes me lie down in green pastures.
> He leads me beside still waters.
> He restores my soul.
> He leads me in paths of righteousness
> for his name's sake. [12]

God gives you many things to enjoy that bring pleasure: food, friends, vacations. But they will never satisfy your deepest appetites. Like Adam and Eve we can forget that.

Which brings me back to church. That's why we assemble. That's why we preachers preach. And although there is a struggle for your attention, we'll keep preparing the table.

Next time you feel those hunger pangs remember that there is bread within reach. Try letting God captivate you.

And may your soul be restored.

Chapter 7

ME-nough

In September of 1957, some moviegoers in Fort Lee, New Jersey, paid more to see their movie than they expected.

They had come to watch the film *Picnic*. Little did they know that James Vicary was in the projection booth, prepared to add his own contribution to the fried chicken and watermelon spread out on the screen. He had placed a tachistoscope—a device that displays an image for a specific amount of time—in the booth. Throughout the movie, about every five seconds, he would flash a couple of pictures. One picture said "Drink Coca-Cola." The other said "Hungry? Eat popcorn."

Vicary reported that the results of his experiment were an 18.1 percent increase in Coca-Cola sales and a 57.8 percent jump in popcorn sales. You wonder if anyone saw much of the movie since they were stampeding to the concession stand.

Following his lead, radio and television stations began airing subliminal commercials in an effort to send the public on a mission to acquire things they did not necessarily need only because they saw something that told them they did.[1]

Those New Jersey moviegoers weren't the first to fall for this gimmick. Adam and Eve were going about their business in the garden with everything they needed and wanted until the day the serpent slithered in with a not-so-subliminal thought: "Did God actually say, 'You shall not eat of any tree in the garden'?"[2]

Eve had not really thought about it. God had given the humans fruit and food of all kinds. He had given them one command: "Don't eat from the tree in the middle of the garden." They had been fine with this. So far, God had supplied what they needed. He was trusted.

But something snapped at that point. A thought flashed for a millisecond onto the screen of her mind: "Maybe we are missing out. Maybe we need more. Maybe there is something to that fruit that we need to experience." That's when it happened. "So when the woman saw that the tree was good for food, and that it was a delight to the eyes, and that the tree was to be desired to make one wise, she took of its fruit and ate."[3] She saw the fruit, reached out, and took it.

You and I have done the same. The car you are driving is perfectly fine. It starts when you turn the key. It gets you from home to work and back again. Best of all, it is paid for.

But then you see the commercial. A new vehicle is being rolled out on the screen in front of your eyes. You can smell the new car interior. You see dollar signs as you reflect on the gas money you will save by driving a hybrid, not to mention the applause you will receive for driving "green." But what reels you in are the smiles on the people in the commercial and the numerous friends looking at the car. You get the message: drive this car and you will be happy and have more friends.

Suddenly you see this car everywhere you go. It must be a sign from God that this is something you must have. And before you know it you have signed away five years worth of payments that you were not making while driving your perfectly adequate, debt-free car.

You saw it. You reached out for it. And you took hold of it.

Then it took hold of you. The serpent, let me remind you, is more adept than any advertiser. The advertiser merely wants you to buy the car. The adversary, however, wants you to want. Want a new car. Want a new house. Want a new spouse. He knows you. He knows that if you see something then the possibility is created for you to look somewhere other than God for what you want. And when you do that, bad things tend to follow.

The sequence is repeated throughout Scripture. One evening King David was walking on his rooftop. Notice what happens:

> In the spring of the year, the time when kings go out to battle, David sent Joab, and his servants with him, and all Israel. And they ravaged the Ammonites and besieged Rabbah. But David remained at Jerusalem. It happened, late one afternoon, when David arose from his couch and was walking on the roof of the king's house, that he saw from the roof a woman bathing; and the woman was very beautiful. And David sent and inquired about the woman. And one said, "Is not this Bathsheba, the daughter of Eliam, the wife of Uriah the Hittite?" So David sent messengers and took her, and she came to him, and he lay with her. (Now she had been purifying herself from her uncleanness.) Then she returned to her house. And the woman conceived, and she sent and told David, "I am pregnant."[4]

Understand that David had eight wives and a bunch of concubines. He had plenty of women in his life already—more women than he had days of the week for. Maybe more than he had days in the year for.

But then he *saw*. Some want to blame Bathsheba for bathing in a public way. You have to understand that David does not get out of his responsibility so easily. First, David should have been off at war with the other men instead of lazing around Jerusalem. Second, baths were set on the roofs so that the water could heat up during the day. Bathsheba does not expect to be seen, especially not in the spring by the king who should be off at war.

David sees. Then he sends for her. Then he sleeps with her. Then he pays for it. From this incident forward, David is never the same.

His kingdom falls apart. His family disintegrates. And although loved by God, he pays for the consequence of his actions.

What you see is often what you get. We go after the things we see. Satan knows this. And so he places things in our path that will detour us off the straight and narrow.

So serious is his strategy that Jesus once said, "And if your eye causes you to sin, tear it out. It is better for you to enter the kingdom of God with one eye than with two eyes to be thrown into hell . . ."[5] Jesus' language, although figurative, is strong. Take care in what you see because it can lead you astray.

I know. I once entered a den of iniquity myself. I entered on a mission: find the fruit section of the supermarket. The plan was to eat more healthily. The targeted supermarket, like most, displayed all the healthy basic foods around the perimeter: vegetables, fruit, breads, dairy products. I could make a quick sweep around the store and be exiting toward a healthier heart in record time.

That's when I saw the "aisles of *o*'s." Tucked away in the middle of the store, the aisles of *o*'s are strategically placed so they can be seen from almost anywhere. And these aisles alone can destroy you. Think you haven't been there yourself? Think again. The aisles of *o*'s—Dorit*o*s, Cheet*o*s, Tostit*o*s, Cheeri*o*s, Frit*o*s—an endless array of aisles topped off with the one temptation most difficult to resist—the *Double Stuf Oreos.*

Before seeing them, all I was thinking about were bananas and bread, asparagus and apples. But they sit there quietly calling out, "You want Oreos, don't you?" And my reply is, "Yes! I do! I do want Oreos!" I see. I reach. I take.

Marketers do not even have to resort to subliminal messages. In fact, they believe that their commercials do not really have that much of an effect on us by themselves. Instead, they understand that it is the pervasive message of "buy" that gets us the most. There is always more so you will always need to keep buying to get what you don't have. Once you start consuming, you will become a consumer addict.

Don't think we are that susceptible to advertising? Then look at what happened to the Gwich'in tribe of Alaska.

In 1980 the Gwich'in tribe of Alaska got television, and therefore massive advertising, for the first time. Satellite dishes, video games and VCRs were not far behind. Before this, the Gwich'in lived much the way their ancestors had for generations. Within 10 years, the young members of the tribe were so drawn by television they no longer had time to learn ancient hunting methods, their parents' language or their oral history. Legends told around campfires could not compete with Beverly Hills 90210. Beaded moccasins gave way to Nike sneakers, and 'tundra tea' to Folger's instant coffee.[6]

Marketers are not evil. They are only doing their job (and if marketing moved you to purchase this book, then it has served a very worthwhile purpose). But the point is that we need to be cautious about what we look at for more than a glance. Once seen, anything can become a want. The fruit was just fruit, but Eve saw it and it was "pleasing to the eye." *Pleasing* is translated from a Hebrew word that means *desire, lust, wish, longings of one's heart.* It also means to *covet.*

Covetousness is wanting or wishing for or longing for that which we don't have. Its negative effect on our lives is strong enough to warrant its presence in the Ten Commandments.[7] "Wanting" starts small—"Just one more (fill in the blank) and I'll be satisfied," we say. But then we have what it is we think we want and it quickly loses its allure.

It's kind of like looking around at the Louvre. We were following our maps like sleuths following their clues—a couple of more turns and then we would meet her at our predetermined rendezvous. She would be waiting for us in this hall.

Sure enough, she was. We ventured across the room, slowly making our way through the crowd of people who had also hoped to see her. When we saw her, she was not quite what we expected:—small, old, not very beautiful; barely a smile on her face.

The Mona Lisa did not deliver. We looked at her for a few minutes and then moved on. The crowd demanded that we not keep her for ourselves. We left, feeling grateful to have seen her, but quickly ready to move on to the next masterpiece.

Maybe that is what David experienced. He had experienced other women. But he thought he needed another. Adam and Eve had tasted plenty of fruit. But they thought they needed one more. Every time we acquire something new it does not take long for the new to wear off. Suddenly our old moccasins seem outdated. There might be a better fit out there somewhere.

The problem is not with what else is out there. The problem is what is in us. The ME-addiction. The disease that causes us *dis*-ease. We are restless and keep searching for something to give us peace. Jesus says it will never be found in things.

> Therefore I tell you, do not be anxious about your life, what you will eat or what you will drink, nor about your body, what you will put on. Is not life more than food, and the body more than clothing? Look at the birds of the air: they neither sow nor reap nor gather into barns, and yet your heavenly Father feeds them. Are you not of more value than they? And which of you by being anxious can add a single hour to his span of life? And why are you anxious about clothing? Consider the lilies of the field, how they grow: they neither toil nor spin, yet I tell you, even Solomon in all his glory was not arrayed like one of these. But if God so clothes the grass of the field, which today is alive and tomorrow is thrown into the oven, will he not much more clothe you, O you of little faith? Therefore do not be anxious, saying, "What shall we eat?" or "What shall we drink?" or "What shall we wear?" For the Gentiles seek after all these things, and your heavenly Father knows that you need them all.[8]

Those who do not follow Christ follow a different formula. Theirs is: "Let's get all the things we want and then add God." Those who follow Christ follow this formula: "Let's get God and we will have everything we need." Jesus put it this way: "seek first the kingdom of God and his righteousness, and all these things will be added to you."[9]

David knew the truth of life even if he failed to follow it at times. "The LORD is my shepherd; I shall not *want* . . ." he wrote.[10] Can you say the same?

Jean Kilbourne—recognized internationally for her pioneering work on the image of women in advertising—writes that "The story that advertising tells is that the way to be happy, to find satisfaction—and the path to political freedom, as well—is through the consumption of material objects."[11] It's the same story the serpent told. Something more will make you happy.

And it's the same lie that Vicary gave. He later admitted that there was not enough real data to prove his subliminal message technique, but for a time he was believed enough to warrant study after study and the eventual banning of this practice.

Vicary was right. These messages do not have to control our cravings. It's not the messages we see that we need to be concerned about, it's those that are within. Later studies have indicated there is something to subliminal messaging. They can have an effect on a person if that person were already predisposed to being thirsty, hungry, etc.[12]

So do not panic. Subliminal messages do not have to control your life. And more importantly, you do not have to be controlled by the enemy's messages either. You don't need more popcorn or soda, cars or clothes. You need more of God. You need a transformation in your predisposition.

So Jesus offered another story when he said there is one thing only that will bring you joy. "The kingdom of heaven is like treasure hidden in a field, which a man found and covered up. Then in his joy he goes and sells all that he has and buys that field."[13] If you are going to reach for something, reach for the kingdom of God. You'll have everything you need.

Next time you see a new product or another commercial or another man or another woman, stop and see Jesus instead. Turn your heart to him. Recall the verses of Scripture we have discussed. Turn your eyes away from whatever else is vying for your attention.

You'll find yourself wanting less. And you'll find yourself having more. What you have in God is greater than anything you don't have in life.

Chapter 8

The ME-Ego

"Pride goes before destruction, a haughty spirit before a fall."[1] John Sedgwick should have heeded this piece of wisdom from Proverbs. During the Battle of the Wilderness in the Civil War, John Sedgwick, a Union general, was inspecting his troops. At one point he came to a parapet, stopped, and looked out over it in the direction of the enemy.

His officers suggested that this was unwise and perhaps he ought to duck while passing the parapet. "Nonsense," snapped the general. "They couldn't hit an elephant at this dist—" A moment later Sedgwick fell to the ground, fatally wounded.[2]

Thinking we know more than we know can be harmful at the least, deadly at the worst. Take the young son, for example. Everything he needed was there: a roof over his head, food enough to fill a feast, clothes from the latest designers and, most importantly, a wise and loving father. He knew his home like the back of his hand.

And maybe that was the problem. He thought there might be more. Having spent his life within the protected walls of his parent's house, he began to think there might be something his father knew but wasn't telling him. So he set out on his own.

Before he knew it, he did know more. He knew that friends can vanish as quickly as money disappears. He knew about poverty.

He knew about pigs. He knew about pride. And since he'd rather swallow his than swallow pig slop, he headed home to his father.

The story of the prodigal son has been called the greatest short story ever written, perhaps because in one form or another, it is everyone's story. It is a retelling of our story that began in the garden. *Adam* is the name depicting the first man *Adam* is also the Hebrew word meaning *humankind*. So this story found in Genesis 3 is also our story. Adam and his wife Eve saw something in the fruit that would not let them go. There was other fruit that was "pleasing to the eye," but it was this fruit that caught their eye. They saw an opportunity to gain knowledge that they did not have: the knowledge of "good and evil."

God had that knowledge. Adam and Eve desired it. The difference between them was that God, the Good Father, knew how to handle this knowledge. He could and would only choose good. He had nothing to do with evil. And in his love for humankind he gave them one prohibition: "but of the tree of the knowledge of good and evil you shall not eat."[3]

Did they listen? Do we? There is something in us that has to find out for ourselves rather than trust the Father who knows best.

When our youngest son, Taylor, was about four years old, we were visiting my folks in Arkansas. Their house was a ranch style house. The good thing about that house was a long hallway that took you from one end of the house to the other. The bad thing about that house was a long hallway that took you from one end of the house to the other. Young boys love long hallways. And young boys run like maniacs down them.

One day the boys were pretending to be the Flash or some fast superhero and I had to do what dads do. I stopped them and gave them a mini-lecture. "Boys, you need to stop running down the hallway." Then they did what kids do. They asked, "Why?" "Because you can fall and get hurt" was my answer.

For a few minutes they were fine with that prohibition. Then all of a sudden I heard two little four-year-old feet scampering down the hall again. Before I could move to stop them I heard a sickening "thud." I ran down the hall (I know, I know, I had told them not to, but I'm the dad!). When I got to Taylor I saw he had fallen and hit his head on the corner of a coffee table. I saw blood around his temple area.

When I came to after fainting, I found our six-year-old Kris had cleaned up the blood, was holding a compress to Taylor's head, and was saying, "Dad, here are the directions to the nearest ER." (You almost bought that, didn't you?)

Sound familiar? A father gives a warning to protect his children. The children have to find out the hard way that the father knew what he was talking about. It's the same story that began with Adam and Eve. They wanted the power of knowledge of good and evil for themselves. They wanted to decide for themselves what was right and wrong. They wanted to be their own "gods."

We see it in our children. And we see it in us.

- The Father says to take one day a week to rest.[4] But we know better and work 24/7 and are rewarded with ulcers and anxiety.
- The Father says to learn from the ant and work diligently.[5] But we procrastinate and put off and then find ourselves laid off.
- The Father says to be content with what you have and master your money. So what do we do? We accumulate more on plastic and find ourselves enslaved to consumer debt and interest payments.[6]
- The Father says to put to death sexual immorality, impurity, lust, evil desires, greed, anger, rage, malice, slander, filthy language, and lies.[7] We nod our heads and yet allow these to linger in our lives.

The outcome is the ME-addicted life. We want knowledge apart from God to make our own decisions. Then, when our world crumbles, we run back to God like the prodigal son ran back to his father.

The Scriptures call this desire for knowledge apart from God *pride*. Pride creates some big problems. First, *pride puts us at odds with God.* The Proverbs, which by the way were written to teach us true wisdom or knowledge about life, say:

- "Everyone who is arrogant in heart is an abomination to the Lord; be assured, he will not go unpunished."[8]
- "Pride and arrogance and the way of evil and perverted speech I hate."[9]
- "There are six things that the Lord hates, seven that are an abomination to him:" The first one mentioned? "Haughty eyes," at times translated "a proud look . . ."[10]

Why does God hate this arrogant form of pride so much? Because we were created to reflect his glory. Pride causes a person to glorify himself instead of glorify God. Jesus told the following story about a prideful man:

> And he told them a parable, saying, "The land of a rich man produced plentifully, and he thought to himself, 'What shall I do, for I have nowhere to store my crops?' And he said, 'I will do this: I will tear down my barns and build larger ones, and there I will store all my grain and my goods. And I will say to my soul, Soul, you have ample goods laid up for many years; relax, eat, drink, be merry.' But God said to him, 'Fool! This night your soul is required of you, and the things you have prepared, whose will they be?'"[11]

Did you notice the rich man's words? "He thought to *himself . . .* What shall *I* do? . . . *I* have . . . This is what *I'll* do . . . *I* will tear down . . . *I* will store . . . *I'll* say to *myself . . .*" It's all about him. He does what he wants to do. He does what he thinks is best. He even gets advice from—himself. Not once does he invite the One who made it possible for him to have his wealth into the conversation. Pride pushes God out of the conversation—and God hates to be relegated to the sidelines.

God hates to be on the sidelines of our lives because of the second big problem pride causes. God knows *pride will lead to our downfall.* "Before destruction a man's heart is haughty."[12] "Haughty eyes and a proud heart, the lamp of the wicked, are sin."[13]

Pride is incompatible with the Christian life. Note these stern words from Jonathan Edwards, the great Protestant preacher of the 18th century:

> Pride is the worst viper that is in the heart; it is the first sin that ever entered into the universe, and it lies lowest of all in the foundation of the whole building of sin, and is the most secret, deceitful and unsearchable in its ways of working, of any lusts whatsoever; it is ready to mix with everything; and nothing is so hateful to God, and contrary to the spirit of the Gospel, or of so dangerous consequence; and there is no one sin that does so much let in the Devil into the hearts of the saints, and exposes them to his delusions.[14]

The Bible is clear that arrogant pride leads to our downfall. We think we know all we need to know, but we don't. We can't see everything. We can't outguess everything. We don't have all the information or all the experience for everything that comes our way. We like to appear capable of doing more than we really can. And we want others to think so too.

My airplane friend did. We were in our plane on the way back from Jamaica when a flying bug collided with my head. It's a big target, so I was startled that he was unable to avoid it. I watched him fly off and then began to think.

I thought it was odd to see a flying bug on an airplane. "How did he get here?" "Did he go through customs?" "Did he have a ticket?" He went from one passenger to the next, terrorizing each one. So I kept an eye on this bug flying in the plane.

When we landed I watched him as he deplaned. My little friend was a bit bewildered about where he was. Other flying insects gathered round, looking at him in amazement. His dreadlocks were a dead giveaway as to where he was from. But—how had he gotten to Memphis, Tennessee?—they had to ask.

And he answered. "Well, I flew the entire way. I flew hard. I flew high." They calculated the miles and gasped. He proudly continued, "I knew if I didn't, we might all die. Who knows what would have happened to the plane had I ever stopped flapping my wings?"

He was beginning to sound a bit like a gospel preacher with a reggae lilt. By the end of the conversation he had created quite a buzz.

If it were me, I'd probably take credit for that too. We want to look better than we are. We want to take credit when God is due the credit. When John warns us of pride in 1 John 2:16, he says that the "pride of life" is not from the Father. Here, *pride* is defined as *braggart talk*. And *life* has to do with the resources of life or *wealth, goods*. The pride of life involves bragging about your stuff. Whether it is your knowledge or your work or your accomplishments or your money. Pride says it is all because of you. God gets no credit.

And pride leads to a third problem in our lives. *Pride causes us to compare ourselves to others.* A young woman asked for an appointment with her pastor to talk with him about a troubling sin about which she was worried. When she saw him, she said, "Pastor, I have become aware of a sin in my life which I cannot control. Every time I am at church I begin to look around at the other women, and I realize that I am the prettiest one in the whole congregation. None of the others can compare with my beauty. What can I do about this sin?"

The pastor replied, "Mary, that's not a sin. That's just a mistake!"

Chances are we've all had a few "Mary-moments" ourselves. So what can we do about this sin? That's a good question. The apostle Paul gives us an antidote to pride in Romans 12:3: "Do not think of yourself more highly than you ought, but rather think of yourself with sober judgment . . ." The solution to pride is not a false humility. Paul says that there is a way to think of yourself. Just don't think too highly. God has given you abilities. He has given you knowledge. But he has not given you *every* ability. You do not have *all* knowledge. You need God—and you need others.

Paul gives this instruction in the context of the body of Christ. You are one part of it. You may be a valuable part but you cannot do much by yourself. So know a couple of things. You need to know what you know, and you need to know how you are gifted. Think with "sober" judgment and give the glory to God.

In another of Paul's writings he presents this attitude that we would do well to emulate: "But with me it is a very small thing that I should be judged by you or by any human court. In fact, I do not even judge myself. For I am not aware of anything against myself, but I am not thereby acquitted. It is the Lord who judges me."[15] Paul's advice to us is that we should not care what others think about us. We should not even care what we think about ourselves. What matters is what God thinks.

He likens our daily life to going to court. We are always on trial. Pride keeps us performing so that we can get a good verdict. But the good news is that it is the Lord who judges us. The trial is over. We get the verdict—"not guilty, loved"—before the performance: no more comparisons, no more God-less decision making, no more prideful boasting.

Instead, we boast about God. Our work is about God. Our appearance is about God. Our success is about God. We have something to contribute. God created us for good works, but he gets the glory.

When God gets the glory, pride gets out of the way. We can come back home and get to know him.

And that's the knowledge we wanted all along.

Chapter 9

Excuse ME

It all started with an apple. An Apple II to be exact.[1]

Before *SoBig*. Before the *Love Bug*. Before the *Melissa* computer viruses began being fruitful and multiplying themselves through computers around the world, there was the "Elk Cloner." Trace the history of the computer virus and you will journey back in time until you stand face to face with one man. Rich Skrenta.[2]

During a winter break from high school, Rich hacked away on his Apple II computer and figured out how to launch on-screen messages to his friends' computers through a "boot sector" virus. It wasn't called that back then. There was no name yet because Rich started it.

When the computer would boot up, an infected disk would place a copy of the virus in the computer's memory. Then, when a clean disk was put into the system, a copy would get written onto that disk. The new disk would be passed on to other people, then onto other machines, and then to new locations.

Since then he has repented and gone on to make a positive contribution in the world of computer programming. But years later, after all his other accomplishments, Rich is known best for being the first person to ever "let loose a personal computer virus."[3]

He might find an empathetic friend in Adam. Trace the human condition of sin back to its origins and you will stand face to face with one man—Adam. He let loose a personal human virus—the ME-addiction—that has spread to every other living human since. Except one.

Adam wasn't on a break from high school, but it appears he was on a break from work. He had been put in the garden to "work it and keep it."[4] This was before it was hard work, before there were thorns and thistles and it took sweat to work the land.[5]

I'm not sure what it was like to work the garden in those early days, but I imagine it was easy instead of hard, a joy instead of a burden to work the land. Adam did not wake up on Monday morning with the blues, already beaten down before the week began. And he did not approach Friday with a TGIF relief that he was about to get a break. Every day was a "TGI_____ day." Whatever it was like, it was a pleasure and a team effort, where the ground was working with him instead of against him.

Adam's job description was simple: "Work the land." That's it—along with one other piece of command about another matter: the trees. There were two special trees in the garden. The tree of life and the tree of the knowledge of good and evil.

God told Adam that he could eat of any of the trees in the garden—including the tree of life—but he could not eat of the tree of the knowledge of good and evil. He said that if he did, he would die.[6]

Adam heard his job description, slept on it, and woke up with a wife. Talk about getting in touch with your feminine side! His marriage was a match made in heaven, spending his life with the girl of his dreams. But it didn't take long before the honeymoon was over.

At the beginning of Genesis 3 we find the woman hanging out by the trees. A serpent slithered into a conversation with her and placed a virus-infected thought into the dialogue: "For God knows that when you eat of it [i.e. the fruit of the tree of the knowledge of good and evil] your eyes will be opened, and *you will be like God*, knowing good and evil."[7]

The next sound heard was a crunch and humankind has had heartburn ever since.

Remember I said Adam was on a break from work? He was right there by the woman, listening to the entire conversation and never saying a word.

Adam gets the rap for what happened at the trees. In Romans 5:12–21, the apostle Paul says it was through Adam that the ME-addiction came into our world. "Therefore, just as sin came into the world through one man, and death through sin, and so death spread to all men because all sinned . . ."

Adam was there right beside the woman instead of working. She was at the tree instead of helping him work—if he had been working like he should have been, that is. He knew the job description: "Work the land. And eat of everything. Just don't eat of this one tree." This is the Elk Cloner moment of Scripture. This is where the first virus began.

Which raises questions. Ask Rich why he did what he did and he says, "I was in the ninth grade."[8] Ask Adam why he did what he did, and you discover the first excuse ever given: "The woman whom you gave to be with me, she gave me fruit of the tree . . ."[9] Ask Eve why she did what she did and, following Adam's example, she politely excuses herself: "The serpent deceived me . . ."[10]

The ME-addiction brought with it something new to our world: the art of making excuses for our behavior. Before this Elk Cloner moment there had been no need for excuses. Before, there had been perfect trust of God—perfect obedience. But once sin entered our existence, Adam and Eve began making excuses.

Just this week a manuscript that was found in a recent archeological dig came across my desk. It gives new insight into this virus story:

> After creating heaven and earth, God created Adam and Eve. The first thing he said was "Eat." The second thing he said was "Don't!"
>
> "Don't what?" Adam replied.
>
> "Don't eat the forbidden fruit," God said.
>
> "Forbidden fruit? We have forbidden fruit? Hey Eve, we have forbidden fruit!"

"No way!"

"Yes way!"

"Do not eat the fruit!" said God.

"Why?"

"Because I am your father and I said so!" God replied, wondering why He hadn't stopped creation after making the elephants.

A few minutes later, God saw his children having an apple break, and he was ticked. "Didn't I tell you not to eat the fruit?" God asked.

"Uh huh," Adam replied.

"Then why did you?" said the Father.

"I don't know," said Eve.

"She started it!" said Adam.

"Did not!" "Did too!" "DID NOT!"

Having had it with the two of them, God's punishment was that Adam and Eve should have children of their own.[11]

Rich, the creator of the first PC virus, is asked why he started it. He blames it on his age and immaturity. Adam, unskilled at making excuses, saw Eve and figured she was as good as anyone to blame. In fact, she was the only other person he could blame. For extra effect, he also blames God. And Eve blamed the serpent.

It caught on and hasn't stopped. You see this "passing of the buck" in marriages. One of the benefits of marriage is you have someone else in the house to blame. Throw in a couple of kids and everyone is off the hook. Just blame whoever is not in the room at the time and you might get off scot-free.

At times new family members show up. "Who broke the lamp?" you ask. The answers come back: "Somebody else;" "Nobody." You have no clue as to who these people are who apparently live in your house, but they come in handy when you need someone to blame.

Our first parents—Adam and Eve—gave us a pattern we have learned well from and perfected. Jimmy Fallon once said,

"Sometimes I wish I had a terrible childhood, so that at least I'd have an excuse."[12] Just watch kids trying to skip school and you'll hear a litany of bad excuses. The following are real school excuses, explaining the reason behind the absence of students.

- My son is under a doctor's care and should not take P.E. today. Please execute him.
- Dear School: Please ekscuse John being absent on Jan. 28, 29, 30, 31, 32, and also 33.
- Please excuse Tommy for being absent yesterday. He had diarrheea and his boots leak.
- Please excuse Jennifer for missing school yesterday. We forgot to get the Sunday paper off the porch, and when we found it Monday, we thought it was Sunday.
- Please excuse Lisa for being absent. She was sick and I had her shot![13]

Make no mistake, the virus you are being confronted with is more serious than skipping school. Nowhere in Scripture will you find any admonition to make excuses for your sins. Nowhere does Jesus teach us to pray, "give us new excuses for our trespasses, as we listen to the excuses of those who trespass against us."

And nowhere do we find Adam or Eve admitting their wrongs. Seldom do we admit ours, and yet it is the first step in being freed of the ME-addiction. The one time we should focus on ourselves is the one time we don't. When we do something we know to be wrong and are caught is the one time we do not like being the center of attention.

How do we deal with it? We throw "grenades." In dealing with personnel issues over the years, one wise elder would say, "He's just throwing grenades." At first I did not understand. When I asked him to explain, he said, "Well, what happens when someone throws a grenade? People look away to where it lands and explodes. So what I mean is that, instead of just owning up to his responsibility, he is throwing grenades—trying to get us to look somewhere else."

God does not fall for grenades—and he doesn't much like our excuses. He would much prefer us to follow Jesus than Adam. In Romans 5 the Apostle Paul traces the sin virus back to Adam.[14] Then he says, "For as by the one man's disobedience the many were made sinners, so by the one man's obedience the many will be made righteous."[15] That "one man" is Jesus Christ. We've followed the first Adam long enough. It might be a good idea to follow the second Adam instead.

Jesus teaches us a path to follow that will eventually eliminate our excuses. Adam's first mistake was not doing what he was supposed to be doing. He should have been working the land. Eve would have been by his side. Instead, they were both hanging out near the prohibited tree. The serpent found a window of opportunity for his malware to infect.

Notice how Jesus' life differed. In John 5:19 he states: "Truly, truly, I say to you, the Son can do nothing of his own accord, but only what he sees the Father doing. For whatever the Father does, that the Son does likewise." The first step in eliminating excuses then is a preventative one: Be doing what you should be doing. Get your daily plan from God.

Then trust God. Trust that what God directs you to do and warns you to stay away from is good for you. Jesus did. The writer of Hebrews reminds us that "Although he was a son, he *learned* obedience through what he suffered."[16] The word for *learned* is the same word from which we get the word *disciple*. Jesus let God's word and ways be his teacher. Not once did he go his own way.

The word also carries with it the idea of becoming accustomed to or in the habit of something. Jesus' life teaches us that as we trust God continually more, trusting him also becomes more of a habit. It becomes the thing we more naturally do.

But it isn't that way now. And so we need to confess. Jesus' closest disciple, John, gave us this "needs to be highlighted and memorized" verse out of 1 John 1:9: "If we confess our sins, he is faithful and just to forgive us our sins and to cleanse us from all unrighteousness."

Camp out on the word *confess* for a moment. *Confess* is a compound Greek word made up of *homo* and *logeo*. Here's how it breaks down: *homo* means "the same" and *logeo* means "to speak." Put them together and it means "to say the same thing as another, to agree."

When we confess rather than make an excuse, we agree with God that what we did was not in agreement with his word. And John, the closest friend of Jesus, learned that Jesus is willing to forgive us. Unlike people we encounter in this life who may be unwilling to forgive us and free us to learn and grow, Jesus' main concern is that we learn to agree with God in our words and then ultimately in our lives.

Confession eliminates the need for excuses. It allows us to own up to our failures toward God and toward each other. It may even help you eliminate viruses from your life. The New Testament church seemed to assume that if someone was sick it might have been due to a sin that was separating that person from the full flow of redeeming life. So James writes, "Therefore, confess your sins to one another and pray for one another, that you may be healed. The prayer of a righteous person has great power as it is working."[17]

Unconfessed sin can be a special kind of burden to carry in life that may affect us physiologically. Excuses do not help remove that burden, only confession does.

Watch for the ME-addiction next time you mess up. You'll see it when, instead of owning up to your bad decision, wrong action, or—let's just say it—sin, you blame someone or something else and make excuses. (Interesting, isn't it, that we want to be our own "god" but we aren't even big enough to own up to our own failures?)

But once you see the addiction you can do something radical. Instead of relying on yourself, instead of blaming, instead of making another excuse, you can toss the apple down and return to the core of life. Go to God.

He will erase the virus. He'll reboot you to a new life—a life where, when you blow it, instead of blaming, you merely reboot and confess. God will grant you forgiveness and "cleanse you from all unrighteousness." He'll debug the ME-addiction virus in you and clean out your operating system.

Then he will watch to see what good is spread.

Chapter 10

Find ME

If you listen carefully you may be able to hear the faint sound of his shoulder brushing up against the low hanging limbs in the garden.

If you look real close you may see the outline of her once-innocent body as it moves through the thick underbrush.

The two are hiding. Shame and guilt have sent them scrambling into the denseness of the trees. Maybe their secret can be hidden there and only they would know.

One moment the fruit looked so enticing. It promised something: a fuller knowledge of life. The next moment they did know more—more about shame, more about guilt. And for the first time, they knew fear.

So they hid. And Adam's family has been hiding ever since.

Just ask Frank Warren. In November of 2004, Warren printed up three thousand self-addressed postcards. He handed them out at bus stops and stuck them in the pages of library books. The postcards came with these instructions: "Write on the postcard a secret. Something true and something that had never been told to someone before." Then, the postcards were mailed back to Frank's house.

He collected the returned postcards and put them together for an art exhibit in Washington, DC. He figured that after the exhibit was over, the postcard experiment would end. But the secrets kept coming.

People from all over the United States and even around the world have posted their secrets on Warren's website, PostSecret. com, which has ranked as high as the seventh most popular blog on the internet.[1] Four by six inch cards are created and anonymous participants cut and paste pictures, draw and paint their secrets and send them to Warren, who then posts a number on his website each week. In three years he received over 150,000 secrets.

One of his favorite cards is one he has never seen. A woman e-mailed him and revealed she had been to the website, purchased a postcard, had carefully chosen her words, and decorated her card. She thought she'd feel better but the experience made her feel terrible, so she tore up postcard and decided at that moment to change her life.[2]

When Warren was asked what he has learned from his art he noted two things: "the power secrets have over us and the ability we have, with a simple act of courage, to take back that part of our life and take ownership of the secrets that we have been hiding for so long."[3]

Secrets shared have ranged from regrets to hopes, funny experiences, unseen kindness, fantasies, fears, betrayals, erotic desires, feelings, confessions, and childhood humiliation.[4] Warren receives e-mails from people telling him that facing their secrets on postcards and releasing them to strangers is therapeutic for them. It is better than keeping the secrets to themselves.

The PostSecret experiment indicates that a lot of people in America have something to hide. The only problem with PostSecret is that people share a secret in a secretive way. No one signs their name. No one other than Frank gives their address. They can share their secret but remain in hiding.

But Adam and Eve cannot. They are found out by God. They have followed their own way, and yet God calls out to them. A few moments earlier they turned the command of their creator into an option. Even though God created them, even though he had given them all they needed, they went their own way.

When they did they wound up in hiding—anxious, full of fear, and full of guilt. Their answer to their anxiety is described in the story by Adam and Eve hiding among the trees of the garden.

> And they heard the sound of the Lord God walking in the garden in the cool of the day, and the man and his wife hid themselves from the presence of the Lord God among the trees of the garden. But the Lord God called to the man and said to him, "Where are you?" And he said, "I heard the sound of you in the garden, and I was afraid, because I was naked, and I hid myself."[5]

The reason they hid? "Then the eyes of both were opened, and they knew that they were naked."[6]

What a strange comment: "and they knew that they were naked." Just say the word and we get a little uncomfortable. Middle school kids start snickering. Others of us are more mature. We hear *naked* and we conjure up some mental picture. (You may need to stop the conjuring and pay attention!)

But if you read the Bible the way it was intended to be read, you watch for words that stand out as important words. And one way you find the important words in a section of Scripture is noting whether or not it is repeated.

Hid is repeated twice. *Naked* is repeated four times. These words move the story forward and create the tension in the story. Moments earlier, they were naked "and not ashamed."[7] Moments later, they are naked and hiding because they are afraid. They are ashamed of their nakedness, and they hide.

It's hard to imagine a place where people walk around without any clothes on and are not ashamed. Just think what would happen if someone walked into a birthday party wearing only their birthday suit. Even if a toddler got loose from a diaper change and ran through the middle of a crowd stark naked, we might think it was cute, but the parent would frantically be trying to catch the child and immediately slap another diaper on their backside.

We say people who hang out on nudist beaches "have no shame." We think "streakers" are funny for a moment, but they usually "end" their run surrounded by people with badges or people in white suits. And, if these funny people are doing something that is really fun, why aren't more of us disrupting sporting events? Or better yet, putting the two together and streaking down a nudist beach?

But that's exactly where Adam and Eve were. They were naked and had no shame. Before you think we are obsessing about this, let me remind you again that the word *naked* is repeated four times in this story. We are meant to hear it and pay attention to it—and understand it.

Don't you relate to Adam and Eve? You get up in the morning and change out of the clothes you sleep in and into your clothes for the day. You never think about getting out of the clothes you sleep in and walking out the front door, do you? You never make a mad dash to the end of your driveway to retrieve your newspaper just to see if you can do it without getting caught, do you? (But now that the thought is in your head how many of you are going to try it now?)

We understand that if we are naked we feel some sort of shame. This is why women spend so much time finding just the right swimsuit before summer hits each year. We are not comfortable in our own skin, and anyone who seems to be so comfortable that they need little if any clothing, we call an exhibitionist. It's not a compliment either.

We only have to go to Genesis 3 to discover the fact that *naked* is a theme of our lives. The ME-addiction has a huge downside. Adam's family went from being naked and not ashamed to naked and ashamed when they decided to go their own way instead of God's.

When Eve waltzed up to the tree—the one where God had said "don't eat of this fruit"—and made her own decision to grab a snack for herself and Adam, mankind became addicted to ME. No longer was God the center of their universe. No longer was God the one from whom they derived everything they needed. No longer was God the subject of the story of our world.

If you don't believe me, keep reading. "*I* heard . . . , *I* was afraid . . . , *I* was naked . . . , *I* hid . . . , *I* ate . . . , *I* ate . . ."[8]

God is not included in the earlier discussion around the tree. Only the created beings and a serpent are there talking behind God's back, and the result is the same as what happens to us when we live our lives apart from God—we turn from having an unabashedly honest and trusting relationship with him to one that is broken. Before, you could stand naked before God and feel no shame. You had done nothing wrong. And in this text, *wrong* has to do with "not trusting God."

The result is that, in our anxiety, we hide from God.

As soon as we break relationship with God, we know something has gone wrong even if we don't know what it is. Then we begin to do all sorts of crazy things, trying to hide because of our anxiety and our shame and our guilt and our fear.

Adam and Eve did something crazy. They tried to make some clothes. It's the first cover-up. They try to make something they have never seen and apparently don't do a very good job. They make loincloths out of fig leaves. Try wearing some fig leaves some day and see how that feels.

But don't laugh too quickly. We don't fare much better. We hide behind our resumes. We hide behind the make of car we drive. We hide in our jobs. We hide in our constant going. We hide in our cocooning when we get home.

For some, the Bible can be a fig leaf. We go to church. We quote some verses. We leave quickly. We think, "No one will ever look and see what I'm really about." We find our own ways to hide, and they aren't any better than a fig leaf outfit.

We give up all the good that God wants for us and instead turn to others for our self-esteem and our need for love. We cover up our disorder by finding a therapist who will tell us what we want to hear, preachers who will tell us how good we are, make-up that will hide the fact that we are getting older and more wrinkled. We buy larger houses and bigger cars and more clothes in an attempt to feel better about ourselves. We play to the popular crowd so that we can feel right about ourselves.

And some send postcards anonymously to a person they do not even know in an attempt to relieve the guilt of their secrets. Sending in postcards may help for a moment, but we are still left naked. We cannot clothe our secrets by hiding them under our pride or our rationalization or our denials because the truth of the story is we have violated God first before we have wronged anyone else.

That's why God finds his humans in the garden. Adam has decided to hide in the bushes. Now does that strike anyone else as foolish? It's like the two would-be home burglars who dressed in all black attire but then decided that what they really needed to disguise themselves with was a mask of some sort to cover their faces.

No one is certain which of the two came up with their brilliant idea, but they decided that to hide their faces they would just draw a mask on them. With a permanent Magic Marker.

After a witness saw them trying to break into an apartment and called police, the startled criminals took off. The witness described the dynamic duo as having painted masks on their faces and also gave police a description of their getaway car. When the police spotted the car they also found the two criminals. They had no problem identifying them either. They still had on their masks.[9]

Adam's attempt at hiding wasn't any better. It's not like God could not see them hiding in the trees. But instead of handcuffing Adam right then and there, he calls out, "Where are you?" Now understand, God knew where they were hiding. The reason he asks the question is he wants them to know where they are—what their condition is. Adam is hiding behind trees and behind excuses. Everything had started off good, his wife naked and cooking food. Next thing he knows, she is putting clothes on and cooking stuff he didn't ask for. So God lays out the truth of the matter and speaks clearly about what they have done.

And then he makes some designer clothes for them. These garments were made of "skins."[10] Picture the scene. An animal is killed, a first in the history of the world. Adam and Eve watch as God has to put to death something that was dear to him in order to clothe the humans. If they had not understood the severity of their decision to go their own way before, now they might.

To put the new clothes on—ones that had to be much softer and more comfortable and a better fit than their self-made fig leaf creations—they would have had to stand before their creator naked and ashamed. And yet he covered their shame with his gift of clothing for them because their own attempt at doing this had not worked out well. And to do this they had to feel the touch of God on their nakedness. They had felt the fear of God but now felt his gracious touch.

Laugh at Adam all you want, but we are him. Some think the sin they are committing doesn't count because God can't see it.

Your spouse is away and you flirt with someone else because they can't see it. But God does.

You gossip on the phone about someone else. You think no one else can hear. But God can.

Teenagers hide what they are doing from their parents. But God sees.

Some hide pornography under their mattresses as if God can't see through the springs. Or they just look online as if God does not know how to use a computer. Our attempts at hiding are just as laughable as Adam's.

In the New Testament, there is a story about a son who decides he knows better how to live his life than his father does.[11] So he goes his own way and after a period of living life to the full, he hits rock bottom. His friends are real pigs.

So he goes home. Dressed in rags for clothes, he had not done too well on his own. But his father sees him coming, and the first thing his father does is cover him with a robe, a robe that hides his mistakes and his shame from others and restores their relationship.

Maybe you need to go home too. God is calling to you too. He has watched as someone dear to his heart—his one and only son—was put to death so that our sin could be covered. Maybe that's why the writers of the New Testament are so adamant that we understand our nakedness and what God wants to do for us. Replace *sin* in the passages below with *Me-addiction* and feel the impact:

- "If we say we have no sin [ME-addiction], we deceive ourselves, and the truth is not in us. If we confess our sins [ME-addiction], he is faithful and just to forgive us our sins [ME-addiction] and to cleanse us from all unrighteousness."[12]
- "Therefore, confess your sins [ME-addiction] to one another and pray for one another, that you may be healed. The prayer of a righteous person has great power as it is working."[13]
- "For all of you who were baptized into Christ have clothed yourselves with Christ."[14]

When we attempt to hide our sin, our sin secrets have a power over us. They leave us feeling naked and ashamed, anxious and fearful. We try make-up and cover-ups to hide our slip-ups.

What will you do with your secrets? You can write them on a postcard and send them to a man that has his own secrets, just like you. You can run and try to hide from God.

Or you can run to God. Come out of hiding and let God change your life. He'll remove your fig-leafed ME-addiction and replace it with his grace. You can be clothed in Christ today.

With that perfect fit you can come out of hiding.

Chapter 11

ME & Family

The eighth grade provided me with an opportunity to either do well or not do well.

In San Angelo, Texas, a city-wide speech tournament was held every year for grades seven through nine. Strangely enough for a shy kid, I won in the seventh grade. I basically cleaned up: three first place ribbons, one second place ribbon, and I took home the overall trophy.

The same thing happened in the ninth grade: three first place and one third place. The overall trophy sat in my room for a number of years.

But eighth grade was different. A new kid at our school decided to enter the contest at the last minute. I was a bit miffed that he would dare to tread into my kingdom. I had claimed this territory the previous year. But I also figured every other eighth grader would just lie down and admit defeat as soon as I started speaking.

Not this one. In fact, he won three first place ribbons. He did not enter the fourth category; I won that one, along with three second place ribbons. In previous years they used a point total to decide who won the overall trophy. On points I won. But this year they gave him the trophy on account of his three first place ribbons.

I was angry, very angry, and my countenance fell. But I did my best to hold it together and be a good sport. To add insult to injury, when it was time to go I found that my mother—being the good Christian that she was—had discovered that my enemy needed a ride home. So I had to act like I was happy for him while enduring the ride home with him sitting there holding "my" trophy.

It bugged me that one of the ribbons was for Bible reading. "He probably doesn't even own a Bible" I thought. Then another thought hit me, even in eighth grade. "Yes, but you own one and it says that this is a person that God loves. You love him too."

I didn't want to. A conflicted spirit is the result when thoughts like this hit you in life.

The same thoughts can hit you at church too. They did Cain and Abel. One day they went to church. Actually, the Bible says they each brought an offering to God—but this may very well be the first church service ever recorded.

Cain and Abel were brothers, but like many siblings, they were very different from each other. Cain was the oldest of the two, the firstborn. His job was to work the land. It's the same job description his father, Adam, had adhered to.[1] So he brought God something from the land, "an offering of the fruit of the ground."[2]

Abel was the younger son. Somehow he had become a shepherd, so he brought to God "the firstborn of his flock and of their fat portions."[3] He's working the other part of Adam's job description.[4] So far, so good. A nice time of worship for the boys with their God.

But something happened. God "regarded" Abel's offering, but He did not "regard" Cain's. *Regard* means to *gaze at* or *behold*. There was something about what Abel brought that caught God's eye.

God wasn't the only one who noticed. Cain did too. And because God's response to Abel's offering was more favorable than to his own, he became angry—*very* angry.

Has this ever happened to you? Someone in the family just seems to have the golden touch. Everything they do creates more wealth. Everything they say gets heard. They walk in the room and, like a magnet, people are drawn to them.

But you? It seems no matter how hard you try you cannot get a break. Nothing you do seems to get you anywhere. Nothing you say seems to get noticed. You walk into a room and it's almost as if you are not there.

Or you go to church. You serve, you help, you do everything you can do and it doesn't seem to get noticed. But there is that other person who everyone seems to like, that person who wins friends and influences people and who hasn't ever even read the book.

Surely you've been there before. And if you have, it is an even more difficult pill to swallow if it happens pertaining to things of God. Because then you wonder if God cares about you. You struggle with whether or not he notices you—and you want to be noticed.

Cain surely struggled with this feeling. Especially when God comes to him and asks, "Why are you angry, and why has your face fallen?" I think I'd say, "You don't know?! I brought you what I could bring you. You gave me this work to do and I gave it back to you. I can't help it if you like sheep more than turnips."

But Cain says nothing. He does not deal with his anger. He does not admit that his inner feelings are showing up on his face. So God speaks again: "If you do well, will you not be accepted? And if you do not do well, sin is crouching at the door. Its desire is for you, but you must rule over it."[5]

Let's pause the story for a moment. It appears that it is within Cain's ability to do well. He can respond in a way that is right. Just like his parents, he has a choice. What he cannot do is blame his anger or his envy on anyone else. He can own it.

And he can know that he can be accepted. The simple answer to the question "If you do well, will you not be accepted?" is *yes*. If Cain does well, he will be accepted. Acceptance from God is what he wants. For whatever reason, God gazes at Abel's offering, but it does not mean that Cain is not accepted. He is, if he does well.

Cain is given a strong warning. The first time *sin* is mentioned in the Bible is right here. And sin doesn't enter quietly. It is characterized as a lion or tiger that is ready to pounce on Cain.

Sin has a desire for him and is ready to take him over. But again, he can rule over it. He does not have to let sin have its way with him. He can fight back and not let the lion have him for lunch. This is a huge moment, a moment of no turning back.

It's at that moment that we are tempted to say something about someone else who seems to have something we want. Maybe they get the attention and we don't. Maybe they get the promotion that we wanted. Maybe they got the looks and we got nothing. It's any moment that someone else is preferred over us.

What do we do in those moments? Usually we do our best to knock the other person down a step or two. We want the attention—and we have an opportunity. We can say something about them to make them look bad. We can lash out at them so we can feel better. We feel the urge to correct this injustice. That moment needs to be seen for what it is. "Sin" is ready to make a flying leap and devour us.

Wanda Holloway had sin crouching at her door. In 1991 she asked her brother-in-law to hire a hit-man to kill the mother of a girl who was competing against her daughter for a spot on the cheerleading squad. She thought the teen would be so upset she would drop out of the competition. She was sentenced to serve ten years in prison, served only six months of the sentence, and then spent nine and a half years on probation.[6]

Tonya Harding didn't do much better. Her competition was skating and Nancy Kerrigan was being favored. So Tonya's ex-husband hired Shane Stant to break Kerrigan's leg. He attacked her with a collapsible police baton, only bruised her, but did enough to keep her out of the national championships. Later, at the 1994 Olympics, Harding finished eighth while Kerrigan finished second.[7]

Needless to say, neither of these women did well, and neither did Cain.

Instead of ruling sin, Cain got ruled. Somewhere between his anger and his action he made his choice. He got his brother to go with him to the field. The younger sibling was no doubt excited to be with his big brother even if he did detect a hint of harshness in his voice.

Once there, Cain "rose up" against Abel. The words mean *to become powerful*. He hit his brother. And hit him again—and again. With each stroke the desire of sin took over his body until Abel quit begging him to stop. Abel's body became limp. He fell to the ground. His blood stained the earth a dark red color.

That might have been the end of it, similar to what happens to you and me when we do damage to those around us. We might even feel better for a time—until God shows up asking questions, which is what he did with Cain.

God asked, "Where is Abel your brother?" Not just "Abel." But "Abel *your brother*." Cain said coyly, "I do not know; am I my brother's keeper?"[8]

If God were out of the picture, that question would be much easier to answer. "No, I'm not my brother's keeper. I am a rock. I am an island." But for those of us who recognize God, we cannot escape this question any more than Cain could escape the attention of God, which, by the way, he did get, just not exactly in the way he wished.

The New Testament tells us to "Let love be genuine. Abhor what is evil; hold fast to what is good. Love one another with brotherly affection."[9] New Testament writers like to use different words for *love*. The first love in this verse refers to agape love. It's a love that tells us we must learn to love in the way that God loves. It's the love we are to give no matter how the other person receives it or responds to it.

The second love has to do with the love of a parent to their child, or between husband and wife. It's family kind of love. The writer says to love that way with "brotherly affection." Literally, the term there is "brotherly love"—*philos*, as in Philadelphia, the city of brotherly love.

Agape love teaches us that we are to love in the *way* God loves. Philos love teaches us that we are to love *who* God loves. This was what he had the opportunity to "do well." Cain missed his opportunity to love who God loves. And we do too.

We can agape others by not killing them when we are jealous of them. Let's make something very clear: killing Abel was not a loving thing to do. We can agape people at times by not even being near them because we know we might do something we would regret if we were near them. Cain would have been more loving by just staying away from Abel until he got control of himself.

But philos love will not allow that. We have to get close to people, like brothers, to love in this way. Unless we learn to do that, sin is crouching at the door and will devour us until we, or someone else, is dead.

The same point is made in 1 John 3:11-15:

> For this is the message that you have heard from the beginning, that we should love one another. We should not be like Cain, who was of the evil one and murdered his brother. And why did he murder him? Because his own deeds were evil and his brother's righteous . . . . We know that we have passed out of death into life, because we love the brothers. Whoever does not love abides in death. Everyone who hates his brother is a murderer, and you know that no murderer has eternal life abiding in him.

There's no escaping it. Whether you are at a family gathering or church gathering or community gathering, you have "brothers and sisters." There may be little resemblance in your features. Your character may be light years different than theirs. But you have only to answer one question to realize you are related: "Who does God love?

That's a question you won't ask if you are ME-addicted. The addiction to ME wants not just *some* attention but *all* of the attention. It causes us to create our own kingdoms where we rule and have a desire to expand that rule. Which becomes a problem when we bump up against someone else who has their own kingdom and takes a cut of ours.

In this case, Abel took a cut of the attention that Cain wanted for himself. In your case it could be anything. Whatever it is, you suddenly feel threatened. The ME in you rallies the troops to defend your borders. And instead of "doing well," you do anything but well and someone gets hurt.

You see that other person as the enemy who must be defeated at all cost, instead of someone God loves. Someone who is your brother or sister, who is the one we are to love with an up-close, face-to-face kind of brotherly love. Just as God called Cain to be involved in a positive way in the lives of those in his family, God calls us to care for those around us as we would—or at least as we should—our own family.

The truth is, it is not always easy, especially when that person gets the attention we would like to have. And that is exactly the reason we need God. We think we don't need him. We think we can do well without him. But just try to love your neighbor as yourself. Go ahead. See how well you do. It's not easy, is it?

- It's not easy when you've worked hard for twenty years, only to see the promotion go to a younger co-worker with a degree that was not even awarded when you were in college.
- It's not easy when you serve quietly away from the spotlight, only to see it shine on someone with a more extroverted personality.
- It's not easy when you are part of a team on a project and yet the leader gets all the accolades.
- It's not easy when anyone gets something you want and you feel left out and you need to react in some way other than anger or anxiety or retaliation.

You can't really love someone else when you love yourself most. The ME-addiction creates selfish desires inside us that are waging their own battles. "What causes quarrels and what causes fights among you? Is it not this, that your passions are at war within you?"[10] Those internal wars erupt into external wars. No wonder we fight. And argue. And even kill.

On your own it is nearly impossible to do well. It is difficult to be reconciled with others. But with God, all things are possible.

That's when these words become important. That's when these words show us how Me-addicted we are. We are to love the people God loves, and we can't if we are concerned most about ourselves. We have to replace the ME-addiction in us with a diligent effort to yield to the Spirit.

God calls out to us to be near our brothers and sisters and love in a brotherly way. Too often we would rather attack or retreat. That is when we most need God. Loving him will move you to love others. The answer to Cain's question, "Am I my brother's keeper?" is *yes*.

The word for *keeper* is the same as the word used for Cain's father Adam's vocation. He was to "keep" the garden. Cain followed in his steps but lost sight of the other keeping he was to do. The more *important* keeping he was to do. He was to nurture and care for his brother more than the land.

In our daily grind of work, do we do the same? In our ME-addicted approach to work, do we forget that God has called us to love those whom he loves? Could it be that the work he has given us is merely a vehicle to put us in proximity with those we are to "keep"? Try seeing those people as brothers and sisters and love them in the way God would.

If you don't, you might find yourself being devoured by sin.

I still have all those ribbons from junior high. I also have a newspaper clipping announcing the results of the speech tournament from my eighth grade year. If you could see it, you would see that on the line that states who won the overall trophy for the eighth grade I had crossed out my opponent's name and written mine in instead. I didn't do too well at that time.

But you can. You can do well. You can do well at family gatherings and you can do well in worship and you can do well during the week.

And if you do, others may or may not notice.

But you can be sure that God will.

Chapter 12

Living ME-Free

Hopefully by now you are convinced that you have a ME-addiction. And hopefully along the way you have found some things that are helpful. But now it is time to give you the one thing that will most help you eliminate the ME-addiction in your life.

But first a story.

In 2008 I was given a three month sabbatical from my ministry duties at our church. My family and I were fortunate to travel to Paris, through Germany, and then to Italy. Most people target Venice and Florence and Rome for their Italian stops. We did see Venice and Rome, but in-between we stopped in Parma.

Parma is home to Parma ham and Parmesan cheese. It is also home to Panthers. The Parma Panthers are an American-style football team in the Italian professional league. They gained notoriety in the book *Playing for Pizza* by John Grisham. I had read the book and since the Panthers were in season when we were planning to be in Italy, Parma made our itinerary.

The plan was to actually attend a game, but because we made a wrong connection on a train, we arrived too late. As it turned out, it didn't matter. As we checked into our hotel, we learned that the game date had been changed and they had played it the day before. (Not quite the NFL.) But our hotel clerks said they would "see what they could do." After all, we were the first guests at their hotel who had claimed they had come to Parma solely due to the book.

The next morning we went out to explore Parma. When we came back to the hotel, the clerk, Luigi, (I'm not making that up!) had an e-mail for me. It was from Ivano Tira, the president and owner of the Parma Panthers. He said that he would come by the next evening, pick me up, and take me to one of their practices. The Italian teams practice in the evenings because most of the players work jobs for a living and play for—you guessed it—pizza!

Sure enough, Ivano appeared as planned and I met players, watched practice, ate pizza and returned to the hotel at 2:30 a.m. A friendship was established. Later that year, Ivano and his wife came to the United States and attended a Texas A&M game with me and a friend.

Why the story? Why can I get so excited about the Parma Panthers and you don't? Because I have been face to face with the owner! I have a Panther shirt, I have a Panther banner, and the Panther owner and I are in communication on a regular basis.

Something changes when we spend time with someone face to face: we begin to look like them.

It happened with Moses. In the thirty-fourth chapter of Exodus, Moses climbed a mountain for a staff meeting with God. God told him to chisel out two tablets of stone and bring them to the summit meeting. Mind you there were no laptops or iPads or netbooks in those days. So Moses brought a couple of tablets of stone. God brought the writing utensil—his finger.

When the meeting was adjourned Moses went back down the mountain. Here are the meeting notes: "When Moses came down from Mount Sinai, with the two tablets of the testimony in his hand as he came down from the mountain, Moses did not know that the skin of his face shone because he had been talking with God."[1]

The tablets of stone were not the only things chiseled. Moses' face had been buffed to a nice shine. Being in God's presence changes a person.

Jesus' face was changed on a mountain too (there might be a pattern emerging here). In Mark 9 we read:

> And after six days Jesus took with him Peter and James and John, and led them up a high mountain by themselves. And he was transfigured before them, and his clothes became radiant, intensely white, as no one on earth could bleach them.[2]

The Greek word for *transfigure* is *metamorphoo*, from which we get our word *metamorphosis*. We see a cocoon and know that a caterpillar is changing into a butterfly. A metamorphosis is taking place. Jesus changed in appearance. Why? For the same reason Moses' face changed: He was in the presence of God.

"Okay, but that was Moses and Jesus, the two big guys of the Old and New Testaments. Things like that are supposed to happen to them." You have a point. But consider Stephen in the book of Acts. We meet him in chapter six. Here's how he is described: "a man full of faith and of the Holy Spirit."[3] Not the leader of people out of Egypt, not the Son of God himself; he's just a man, a man who happened to have faith and God's Spirit. And because he did some great things and told others about God, he was captured by the religious leaders and brought to their religious court.

I'd have been shaking in my boots, if I had any boots. I would have been thinking about ME and my self-preservation. I would have been scared silly and looked like I was facing a firing squad. But Stephen? "And gazing at him, all who sat in the council saw that his face was like the face of an angel."[4]

Still not convinced? You think Stephen was a special case because he was one of the first-century believers? Then listen to the words of Paul: "And we all, with unveiled face, beholding the glory of the Lord, are being transformed into the same image from one degree of glory to another. For this comes from the Lord who is the Spirit."[5]

Did you see the word *transformed*? It's the same word translated as *transfigured* in the story about Jesus on the mountain, and it is a word used about you and me in the word *we*. Paul is unveiling for us some important antidotes to the ME-addiction.

Notice that he tells us we have unveiled faces. The idea is that we can come boldly before the throne of God. Instead of being banished from the garden, God has paved a path for us to approach him, and he wants us to be with him.

Then he tells us we "reflect" his glory. This word has caused quite a bit of commotion. Some interpret it as in a junior high school student using a mirror to reflect the sunlight into someone else's eye so as to annoy that person. (Or maybe just reflecting the light would be more in line with where this is going.)

Other versions translate the word as *behold*, as in someone looking intently into a mirror. You study your face in a mirror. You see the wrinkles. You see the complexion problems. I don't, mind you, but you do. And so you gaze at what you are looking at in the mirror.

Fortunately for those of us who are choice-challenged, the Greek word means both. And both work well because Paul is trying to tell us that, when we look intently at God, we are being transformed into his likeness. Others can see the result on our faces. It happens.

How does it happen? It's important to note that we do not make it happen. We do not change ourselves. I've tried. For years I have stared into a picture of Brad Pitt, hoping for a personal change, but I still come away looking like me. I can not make myself appear more like Brad, even though my wife wishes I could. I can not simply make myself change

But God can. He changes us, just like he did Frank.[6] Frank came to see me at my office one day. His face was weary looking: tired eyes, heavy heart. He described to me a life of addiction to pornography.

The addiction had started with his father. Back in the pre-computer days, his dad would keep a stash of Playboys under his mattress. Whether Frank's mother knew about them or not, he never said. But Frank knew where they were. At that early age a cycle began of sneaking a magazine out of his father's room, poring over it, feeling shame and guilt, repenting, promising never to do it again, making it about three days and then starting the cycle all over.

He then looked me in the eyes and asked, "What can I do to stop? I don't want to be like this anymore."

I told him that honestly his particular addiction had never been a problem for me, but that I definitely understood. Other sins that I had dealt with went through the same cycle and yet never seemed to end—at least not when I tried to change on my own.

I leaned in and said, "I can tell you the one thing that seems to work for me. Do you want to know what it is?"

Frank looked at me for the first time with a glimmer of hope and said, "Just name it and I'll do it."

"Great! Here's what you need to do. You need to not only stop looking at the magazines or websites, you need to put something in their place, find something else to look at. Would you make this promise: for one month read your Bible every day? And just read the gospels and look at Jesus. Study him. Look at him. And then come back and tell me about it?"

Frank agreed. I prayed for him and he left.

About a month later he showed up at my office again. I was a bit anxious about what he might report, but as soon as I saw his face I knew the news was good. He literally looked like a different person.

"It worked!" he said. "I cannot get enough of the Bible and I have little if any desire to look at the porn sites anymore. I actually feel as if I have changed."

You cannot any more change yourself than a caterpillar can cocoon itself and muster enough will power to become a butterfly. It is not our job to make the change happen. It is our job to look at God. In looking at him we will be changed.

The problem is, we look at ourselves more than we do God. Interesting, isn't it, that the first navel-gazers had none? Navel-gazing is the problem with the ME-addiction. We cry the mantra statement of "What's in it for ME?" when we should be asking "What's in it for Him?"

Jesus did. In John 5:19-20 he says: "the Son can do nothing of his own accord, but only what he sees the Father doing. For whatever the Father does, that the Son does likewise. For the Father loves the Son and shows him all that he himself is doing."

Jesus lived the only ME-free life that has been lived. And yet he calls for you to follow. He is leading you on the path back to the garden. He paved that path through his death on the cross. As you follow him and look at the Father, your old self will die off. (That's what following someone who winds up on a cross does to you.)

In its place will be someone new. Peter is a prime example. He wanted to know what was in it for him. Jesus appeared to Peter and the other disciples after his resurrection. They were fishing again. Jesus called to them and they came and ate with him on the beach. He was cooking fish on a "charcoal fire."[7]

Interesting that John would note the charcoal fire. You see, Peter knew the smell of burning coals. He had hung around fires for cooking and fires for keeping warm his entire life. But now, the smell of smoke was different for him. Now the smell of smoke triggered a searing memory in Peter's heart. In John 18:18, Peter had stood beside the same type of fire to warm himself. He had given Jesus a cold shoulder by denying him the first time, and had needed warming. So he joined some others by a fire. He had been more concerned about self-preservation than God-glorification. He wound up denying his Lord three times.

Now on the beach the scene is similar. Jesus asks him three times "Do you love me?" The first two times he asks if he "agapes" him, or loves him unconditionally. The third time he asks him if he loves him like a brother. And each time he gives Peter something to do: "Feed my sheep."

Jesus then tells Peter that when he was older he would be dressed by others and be led places he did would not want to go. The key phrase in Jesus' prophecy are the words "you will stretch out your hands." It was a phrase that commonly referred to crucifixion.

A ME-addicted disciple would have walked away at this point. Instead, Peter walked with Jesus. For a moment he stumbled.

He saw John and asked what would become of him. Jesus just refocused Peter's gaze on God. "If it is my will that he remain until I come, what is that to you? You follow me!"[8]

That's it. Follow him. And Peter did. He shepherded this group of rag-tag disciples into the early church. He shepherded the church through the inclusion of Gentiles. He shepherded the sheep until he stretched out his arms and was crucified upside down by request since he felt unworthy to die exactly as his Master had died.

You can follow him too. Keep your eyes on him. Behold him. Ask the question: "What's in it for Him?"

"What's in it for Him in my work?"

"What's in it for Him in my bank account?"

"What's in it for Him in my words?"

"What's in it for Him at my school?"

"What's in it for Him in my church?"

"What's in it for Him in my marriage?"

As you do, you will change. Ernest changed. You see, once there was a valley where many thousand inhabitants lived.[9] Overlooking the valley was a mountain on whose perpendicular side could be seen the features of a human face. One day, a little boy named Ernest sat listening to his mother tell the story of *The Great Stone Face*. She told him of the legend that promised that one day a man with exactly that face would come and visit their village. This man would be a blessing to those around him.

Ernest wanted to see that day come. So at the end of each day he would sit and gaze at the face for many hours, studying its contours. In many ways the face became his teacher as his thoughts and life centered on the blessing the person with the Great Stone Face would someday be.

Through the years, rumors would circulate that one with a resemblance to the Great Stone Face had indeed arrived in the village. Ernest would rush in his excitement to see the person, only to realize quickly that the rumors were false. This happened again and again, leaving Ernest at once disappointed but also hopeful that another day would bring the living legend to his village.

As he aged, Ernest became well known in his region for his wisdom and care. Then one day, as an old man, a poet came to Ernest's village. Ernest read his works with delight and knew this must be the one who resembled the Great Stone Face!

And yet, just as with times past, when Ernest met the poet, he found that the poet, by his own admission, was not the man. The poet knew that his words did not match his life, and that the one who resembled the Great Stone Face must be a man of integrity.

Ernest and the poet became friends, however. One evening, they took a walk together and stopped, as was Ernest's custom, at a particular place in the open air where Ernest would share life teachings with an assembly of the inhabitants of the valley.

As Ernest spoke of what was on his heart and mind, the poet was able to view both Ernest and the Great Stone Face in the background. Suddenly, with an irresistible impulse, he threw his arms in the air and shouted, "Behold! Behold! Ernest is himself the likeness of the Great Stone Face!"

He had become what he had looked at.

The same holds true for us. As we spend time with the Panthers, we become one of them. And as we look intently at God, he changes us to become like him.

The ME in us slowly fades and the HE in us grows.

And that's an addiction worth having.

Chapter 13

Breaking Free from the Kingdom of ME

Some people will always prefer to look at themselves. Want an example?

Measuring only 14.3 acres in total land mass, it is a small kingdom unto itself. Located in three separate areas in the United States—a part in Nevada, others in Pennsylvania, and Northern California—you can leave the United States and enter the Republic of Molossia.[1] It is considered to be a micro-nation—a "nation within" our nation.

Molossia has its own flag, its own signs, and its own boundary markers. It even has its own tourist attractions. Kevin Baugh is the president, or sovereign, of his own little kingdom. He has developed a space program consisting of model rockets. The basic unit of currency in Molossia is the Valora (plural: Valora), which is divided into 100 Futtrus (plural: Futtrus). The Valora is linked in value to Pillsbury cookie dough. Three Valora has equal value to one tube of cookie dough.

There is a railroad—model sized. The national sport is broom ball. And although his nation is landlocked, Baugh claims a navy which is merely an inflatable boat. You can visit anytime you like.

But although it sounds fun don't think you can move there. He says there is not enough room.

Kevin is one among a number of those who see their land as their own kingdom over which they rule. In fact, he affectionately calls his nation "The Kingdom of Me."

Could we be accused of the same? Do we ever suffer from thinking that our world is really all about *us*, with us in the center, a small kingdom unto itself albeit in the middle of seven billion other residents?

Do we suffer from our own "kingdom-itis?"

We may not have gone to the same extremes as Kevin Baugh but we mostly live our lives as if we are rulers of our own kingdoms. What a surprise it would be, then, to have our eyes opened to another kingdom that surrounds us every day: a kingdom as vast as the expanse of the skies, a kingdom in which we actually live and move because it surrounds us. What if someone were to show up and point us to the reality that what we see and what we can control is but a tiny spot in a larger landscape?

That's what Jesus did. He came to our own little Molossias, not as a visitor to see some tourist attraction, but to live among us. Some, like the sovereign of Molossia, said there was no room for him in this world. But Jesus' desire is to come and make his dwelling among us.

He came and talked about a place to live. He said it was a kingdom ruled by a king. In fact, some of the first words he uttered in his ministry were these: "The time is fulfilled, and the kingdom of God is at hand; repent and believe in the gospel."[2]

With these words Jesus began to open our eyes to what is happening around us, to a kingdom that we don't even see. Sixty times in Matthew, Mark and Luke, he talks about the kingdom of heaven or the kingdom of God. Note that it is not the kingdom of ME he is talking about. It is the kingdom of God, and that kingdom takes center stage in the teachings of Jesus.

Not so in ours. We don't like to talk about an absolute ruler. We like democracy in our personal lives, don't we? We like for everyone to have a vote and we're in favor of putting people in office and taking people out of office. So this idea of giving someone absolute lifetime rule over our lives, our behavior, our decisions, our details . . . well, it seems a bit medieval.

But it is biblical. The Bible speaks of God as our king.[3] A king created the world. With just a word he spoke into existence what we see. He parted seas and rescued his people and set up kings. At times these temporary kings acknowledged the eternal King. One such ruler acknowledged that truth with these words: "his dominion is an everlasting dominion, and his kingdom endures from generation to generation."[4]

And then the wild-eyed people called prophets throughout the Old Testament pages spoke of a time God would usher in a new rule on earth. Something different would happen that would lead people away from ME-kingdoms to His kingdom.

> And they shall be my people, and I will be their God.
> I will give them one heart and one way, that they may
> fear me forever, for their own good and the good of
> their children after them.[5]

Notice that this king is concerned about his subjects. When people come under his rule and reign, it is for their good. This king cares about others. The people looked forward to this king and so the prophets spoke of a coming king, an anointed one—a Messiah.

They were told that their hopes of a king would be realized with a birth in Bethlehem.[6] Baby cries soon turned into the initial cry of his ministry, "The time is fulfilled, and the kingdom of God is at hand; repent and believe in the gospel." People were often bewildered that their king would come as a Nazarene carpenter. Someone like them. Someone approachable. Someone whose main mantra statement was "the kingdom of God."

If God is at all important to you, then so is "kingdom." His kingdom. Not yours. He is all about creating a kingdom. One that looks like heaven on earth. And here's the rub: There is only one king in this kingdom, and once this king appears on the landscape of your life, you either begin living under his rule or you rebel. "How does he appear?" you ask. Probably not like you would expect.

We'd expect him to show up with military might and weapons blazing. We think we'd like him to show up in some overpowering way where we have no option but to submit. But that's not his style.

Mark gives us a story that Jesus told about how the kingdom comes to us and how it grows.

> Listen! A sower went out to sow. And as he sowed, some seed fell along the path, and the birds came and devoured it. Other seed fell on rocky ground, where it did not have much soil, and immediately it sprang up, since it had no depth of soil. And when the sun rose, it was scorched, and since it had no root, it withered away. Other seed fell among thorns, and the thorns grew up and choked it, and it yielded no grain. And other seeds fell into good soil and produced grain, growing up and increasing and yielding thirtyfold and sixtyfold and a hundredfold.[7]

Then Jesus said, "He who has ears to hear, let him hear."[8]

The kingdom enters, he says, not as a nation with armies and weapons but as a farmer of all things. Instead of throwing spears or bullets your way, the farmer chunks some seed at you. Jesus says, you and I are like soil. Sometimes the soil is soft and receives the secrets or teachings of the kingdom. They take root when we pay attention, listen and hear, and produce a crop that comes in the form of joy, peace, patience, and happiness. Some grow thirty, sixty or even a hundred times.

But some of us are like hard soil. We have hard hearts and our soil is crusty and rocky and consequently the seed takes no root. There are some who cannot bear to think there is another kingdom outside their kingdom of ME, where there is someone else who might rule their lives.

I don't know if Jesus meant for us to pay any attention to the math in this parable, but if he did, here's what the story tells us:

three out of four people won't respond to this kingdom. To mimic another ME-addicted character, Darth Vader, "The ME-addiction is strong in these ones."

But one out of four does respond. These say, "I could use a king. I'd like to live in that kingdom." And they want to know more about the kingdom and live by its teachings. Their lives begin to bear fruit.

And to them Jesus says, "The kingdom is at hand." It is here. The kingdom of God is not on a mountain or in a micro-nation. It is all around us. The phrase he uses—*at hand*—means that the kingdom of God is within your reach.

Put this book down for a moment and put your hands out. On second thought, just put one hand out and hold the book with the other hand so you can keep reading. How far away is your hand from you? Not very. That's how close the kingdom is to us. And all we have to do is reach out and receive it. Every single human being on the face of the earth has access to the kingdom of God.

Now some might be threatened by this closeness of God. The burglar who snuck into a dark bar after hours was. He went straight to the cash register. That's when he heard a voice that called out, "*God is watching you.*" He looked all around and saw nothing so he returned to jimmying the cash drawer.

Again, the voice said, "*God is watching you.*"

The burglar looked around and finally saw a parrot in a cage and said, "Oh, hi Polly. You startled me."

"Hey," said the parrot. "My name ain't Polly. It's John the Baptist."

The burglar snorted, "Who in the world named you John the Baptist?"

The Parrot said, "The same guy who named that Rottweiler over there, *God!*"

A true understanding of the nearness of the kingdom of God might change our behavior quickly. But sometimes that behavior change takes time. You may have heard about the children who were lined up in the cafeteria of a Christian-based elementary school for lunch. At the head of the table was a large pile of apples.

The director had made a note and posted it on the apple tray: "Take only one. God is watching."

At the other end of the table was a large pile of chocolate chip cookies. One child whispered to his friend, "Take all you want. God is watching the apples."

Jesus told other stories about the kingdom that speak to this new way of life. He scatters them throughout his teaching like the sower scattered the seed. Here's one more out of Mark 4:26–29:

> The kingdom of God is as if a man should scatter seed on the ground. He sleeps and rises night and day, and the seed sprouts and grows; he knows not how. The earth produces by itself, first the blade, then the ear, then the full grain in the ear. But when the grain is ripe, at once he puts in the sickle, because the harvest has come.

Pay attention to what Jesus says. It's not up to you (a ME-Addicted thought) to make the change in behavior. You don't even know how it works. My grandfather was a farmer so I learned firsthand a little about farming. Papa didn't go to Texas A&M and get a degree in agriculture. He just knew that if he took good seed and put it on good soil, and if he was patient enough, he would have a harvest.

The same is true for a life that is lived in the kingdom of God. Maybe some behavior will change quickly—like a thief who realizes God is watching so he stops what he is doing immediately. Maybe it won't change as quickly—like children who understand to leave the apples alone but take extra cookies. But if you are patient and stay near the Word, good things will happen.

We are so used to living one way in our own little kingdoms that when we discover the new one, it rattles our world like two worlds colliding. It's like that because two kingdoms *are* colliding.

The collision is inevitable. The real issue for you is, which kingdom will rule your life? Will you want to remain the king of your own ME-kingdom? If so, your territory will be tiny, your space program puny. Your boats will fit in your bathtub. Your money might even be your meal.

But if you sense that hasn't been working for you and you are ready for a change, if you can believe that there is another kingdom "at hand," then all you have to do is reach out and live into it.

You can surrender your kingdom to the one that is "at hand." The best part is that you can live under a king who allows you to call him "father." Maybe the greatest of the kingdom teachings is that the king is your father. Remember the prayer that Jesus taught us?

> Our Father in heaven,
> hallowed be your name,
> your kingdom come,
> your will be done
> on earth as it is in heaven.[9]

Jesus taught us to pray our "Father" in heaven, not our "king" in heaven. When the king is your daddy, everything changes. He butters your toast in the morning and tucks you in at night. You need a king who is your father. And when the king is your good Father, you will begin to resemble him.

Hudson does already. Hudson is a pint-sized friend of mine who comes to our church preschool. One month, the school had been collecting canned goods to take to a local ministry that helps feed the poor.

Hudson's grandmother had recently retired and had told him that she would not be able to stop at the toy store as often to buy him a toy because she had quit working and would have to watch her spending.

Her words were processed through Hudson's little five-year old mind and came out in his thinking like this: "Grandma isn't working any more. She doesn't have money to buy me toys. Thus, grandma is poor."

The next day at school he told my wife, Karen, the preschool director, "Mrs. Karen. My grandma is retired and doesn't have any money anymore. Can I take her some food because she's poor now?"

Karen, knowing what was going on, couldn't decide if she should laugh or cry. So she played along. And that day Hudson took home some SpaghettiOs in his backpack for his grandma. (Hudson's grandmother later reported it was one of the best meals she had ever had.)

Hudson's care and provision for his grandmother resembled the Father's care and provision for us. Kings and fathers know how to take care of their children. The question is, "What king will you crown in your life? What father will you learn from?"

You and I will try to crown someone or something king. We may, like Kevin Baugh, crown ourselves. Or we may crown our work, or our money, or our travel—and pleasure-seeking. And if we do, our behavior will remain mostly self-centered. And we will discover that the kings we anoint always stumble and fall and don't work.

But the great news of the kingdom of God is that God came to earth and lived here and did not stumble. He did not fall. His kingdom works. He spoke to the winds and the waves and the demons, and he died on a cross and was raised from the dead and said, "All authority in heaven and on earth has been given to me."[10]

Kings say things like that. And kings do things like give themselves up for others—even on a cross. They care for their subjects and their subjects learn to care for each other.

Unlike Molassia, if you want to enter and live in this kingdom, there is room for everyone. That's not the problem. There is room for everyone to live in this kingdom.

The only problem is that there is only room on the throne of this kingdom for one king. If you cannot see that today, you need to know there will be a day when you will see it clearly.

The early followers of Jesus reminded each other of this through a song they would sing. The words are found in Philippians 2:5–11 and end with this kingdom picture: "at the name of Jesus every knee should bow, in heaven and on earth and under the earth, and every tongue confess that Jesus Christ is Lord, to the glory of God the Father."

There will come a time we will all be gathered around the great throne of God and we will see there is only one king.

It will not be Elvis, the King of Rock.

It will not be Michael, the King of Pop.

It will not be Kevin Baugh, the King of Molossia.

And it most certainly will not be you or me. All eyes will be on him. Even yours. There will be no more navel gazing or star gazing but only Savior gazing.

His kingdom is at hand.

It is that near.

And there is room for you.

Afterword

The ME-Free Revolution

Sometimes I feel sorry for Ptolemy.

He was a brilliant mind back in his time. From his vantage point it looked like everything that happened literally revolved around him—around the sphere he knew as earth, around the people he lived and played with.

The sun followed him by day. The moon, like a magnet, was drawn to him at night. The stars? Well, they seemed to dance circles around him too. With the tools he had to work with, he pictured the world moving in one big, circular motion with us in the center.

But as sincere as he was in his understanding, he was wrong.

Sometimes I feel sorry for the Ptolemy's of our day. From the first words of "me" and "my," our world has been plagued with the ME-addiction. Most disturbing is when this addiction permeates our churches.

Jim Henderson and Matt Casper wrote a book called *Jim and Casper Go to Church*.[1] The book is unique because Jim is a veteran Christian and Matt is an atheist. They visited churches across America to see what Matt's reactions would be.

In an interview about the book Matt was asked this question: "Matt, in a nutshell, what are the primary criticisms you have of the churches you visited?" Matt's reply was to the point:

Too much focus on themselves, too little emphasis on the primary commands of Jesus, the person everyone is supposedly there to worship. If churches focused exclusively on making their attendees better at loving one another worldwide and doing unto others as they would have done unto them, well, wow . . .[2]

"[T]oo little emphasis on the primary commands of Jesus . . ." How did that happen? How did it happen that an atheist can visit our churches and see so clearly what we so clearly miss? That it is all about God and not about us.

Would you agree that it is time for another Copernican revolution? Most likely Copernicus had no idea what he was starting. He was just doing what he was wired to do—study the stars and planets and write down what he understood. And then, after many years of his colleagues prompting him to publish his findings, he did. And then he died.

He never knew the change he made in our world.

And you may never know the changes you can make in your world. But by taking steps to become free of the ME-addiction you can right your world. You can see yourself, not as the center, but as one whose life revolves around the Son, Jesus Christ.

A mentor of mine has a saying: "You are the highest leverage point in any system you are in." What that means is this: you can make a difference. You may not think you can. It is much easier to produce a list of excuses as to why things are the way they are and how you cannot do anything to change them.

That's the ME-addiction talking.

Instead, as you follow Jesus, you stop listening to the ME-addicted voice inside your head and begin listening to Jesus' voice. And when you do, you change. And when *you* change, things around you change.

Your family begins to look different to you. No longer are they there to make your life easier. You are there to serve them.

Your job begins to look different to you. No longer are you there just to make a paycheck. Instead, you see yourself as one of

God's imbedded operatives, there to in some way bless those who work beside you every day.

Your church begins to look different too. Where you once entered as a critic of those greeting you, the volume of the music or the selection of the songs, the length of the sermon or the taste of the communion wine/grape juice, now you enter as one who is there to encourage others and tell God how great he is.

"That's being a high leverage point?" you ask? Sure it is. Let me tell you why. There are other ME-addicted people in each of those scenarios, and their first response is to be focused on themselves. And they will bump up against you and expect you to do the same.

But when you respond in a God-addicted way, their world will be spun on its end. You will *Copernicanize*[3] them into a new way to live. You will send them into disequilibrium and possibly cause them to respond as others did in Copernicus' day. They may get mad. They may even turn on you. But they will eventually see something different. They may even see the truth of a ME-free life.

They will see more joy, more patience, more kindness, more goodness, more faithfulness, more gentleness, and more self-control. Oh—and of course, more love.

Next thing you know their world will be righted too. A revolution will begin, and you can be part of it. Who knows? You may even initiate the revolution.

And don't stop at a local revolution. Go global. Imagine the kind of world we would be living in if it were ME-free.

Poverty would end. U2 front man Bono has often said that this generation could wipe out poverty. It is our "moon shot."[4] How would becoming ME-free help end global poverty related issues? We would live on less so that more could simply live. Sometimes you have to see poverty up close for your world to be rocked enough to realize that having it your way isn't so great after all.

I know. My first real brush with extreme poverty was in a mission trip to Cap Haitien, Haiti. One of my favorite pictures from the trip was taken when a group of us travelled to a remote village to see a well that had been built to bring clean water to the villagers.

On the way we saw a little boy who looked to be about three years old watching us as we passed. His hair had an orange tint to it. His belly was extended. We knew he was more than hungry. One of our guides called him "Ti Chape." He explained that the infant mortality rate was about fifty percent for children under five. "Ti Chape" meant "little lucky one" or "little survivor." Haitian parents often called their children by this affectionate name until they reached the age of five because they knew they might not live that long.

I don't know if he is alive today. I do know that he was not alone in his hunger. More than one million people face hunger on a daily basis. The poor spend up to seventy-five percent of their income on food. A child dies from hunger-related causes every seven seconds.[5] And I do know that for as little as thirty-five dollars a month—maybe the equivalent for one dining out experience for many of us—a child can receive life-giving daily basics.[6]

And what about other issues? Children are trafficked for work and sex every day.[7] In the United States alone estimates are that 293,000 children are at risk of becoming victims of sexual exploitation.[8] That's right here in our own backyard.

Malaria kills 781,000 people each year. Of those, ninety-one percent occur in Africa. The majority of those African deaths are children under five years of age. Two thousand die in Africa every day from malaria. Every forty-five seconds a child dies from this disease. And the most staggering statistic of all? Inexpensive long-lasting insecticide-treated bed nets are the fastest way to prevent malaria infection.[9] For as little as ten dollars, you and I can literally save a life.

Water is a daily crisis for a billion of the world's most vulnerable people.[10] A child dies every fifteen seconds due to a lack of clean water. Think there is not much you or I could do about this crisis? Think again. For just under one dollar, clean water can be provided for one person for one year.

Small changes can make a big impact. Or put another way, small "change" can make a big impact. Consider this chart from Stand for Africa:[11]

What can a dollar do in America?

1. Sit on your dresser as change
2. Get lost in the bottom of your purse
3. Buy a pack of gum
4. Buy an inexpensive cup of coffee
5. Buy a cheap toy in a dollar store
6. Buy a small box of french fries

What can a dollar do in Africa?

1. Pay for a doctor's visit
2. Purchase Malaria cure for three people
3. Feed one child three meals for a day
4. Buy a pair of pants, a shirt and some underpants for a small child
5. Buy enough water for a family of three to drink for a week

"Those issues are not my problem." "There's nothing I can do about them." That's the ME-addiction trying to take over again. No, you and I cannot do everything, but we can do something. We can become concerned about the world outside our little world. As John Stott said so well, "We must be global Christians with a global mission, because our God is a global God."[12]

We can start a ME-free revolution.

Sounds good, doesn't it? It takes the earth 365 days to revolve around the sun. What if you and I spend the next 365 revolving around the Son? Each day asking, "What's in it for Him?" instead of "What's in it for me?"

Copernicus revolutionized Ptolemy's standard teaching of the day.

Jesus revolutionized the way Adam's family was moving.

And you can point others to a new way to live too, one that is ME-free. That is what Jesus was up to. He came to bring heaven to earth. (Remember the prayer he taught?) He came to restore what was lost in the garden. The salvation he brought is about "health, wholeness, and healing."

Salvation itself is not just about ME. It's about God and his purposes for his creation. We are included in his purposes, but his intent for us is not that we merely punch a ticket to heaven and then live a ME-focused life of luxury.

God wants us to live ME-free. Free to live for him. Free to live for others.

Just think, if we become better at loving one another worldwide and doing unto others as they would have done unto them, well . . .

Wow!

ME-Addiction Study Guide

Chapter 1: A ME-Free World

1. Define *ME-addiction*.
2. Describe the thoughts or behaviors that reveal a ME-addiction at work in our lives.
3. Describe some of the subtle differences between living a faith focused on God versus a faith focused on ourselves.
4. Describe the value of centering our lives on God instead of on our own wants, needs and desires.
5. *Challenge*: Living in our culture and world today, it is so easy to use the vocabulary of "real faith" while all the time be hiding a worship of self, comfort and watered down commitment. Are we really ready to center our lives on God by realigning our needs according to His plan for what's best for our lives? Are we really ready to abandon our constant attention to what we want in order to live for His larger mission?
6. *Next Steps*: Discuss some next steps for serving, seeking or centering your life on God.

Chapter 2: The Reason for Being

1. Describe/define what a "relationship with God" is or means.
2. Describe ways God might be experienced, revealed, or encountered in your daily life.
3. Discuss how a relationship with God affects us in positive ways.

4. Identify and describe life's interruptions, commitments or distractions that inhibit or erode a relationship with God.
5. Describe how increasing/enhancing a relationship with God is an antidote to the ME-addiction virus.
6. *Challenge*: We can't remove an unhealthy attachment to ourselves or the world until we achieve a healthy attachment to God. But anytime anyone seeks a closer relationship with God, all the lies and distractions Satan has at his disposal will come up against you. You may think you're smarter than Adam and Eve in the garden ... but let's be honest, you're not. You were made for relationship with God and only in that relationship is there any possible chance you and I will find joy in life and power over the ME-addiction.
7. *Next Steps*: Discuss what it would take to dedicate a portion of each day to seeking/establishing/enhancing a relationship with God in your life.

Chapter 3: A World with Boundaries

1. Describe and list some of important social/emotional/spiritual boundaries in our world or lives.
2. Describe how boundaries enhance our sense of being loved and cared for.
3. Discuss the connection between God's boundaries and discovering God's purpose in our life.
4. Discuss the source and/or reason for human angst and resistance against God's boundaries.
5. Describe how rebellion against God's boundaries is linked to the birth of the ME-addiction in us.
6. *Challenge*: No one wants to admit they're selfish, greedy and self addicted! But the fact is, you and I are tempted to resist the very boundaries we need the most. This world isn't heaven and the boundaries and prohibitions of God guide us to life eternal and blessings in our life right now. We need to discover, understand and live by God's design for life.

7. *Next Steps*: Describe specific steps you might take next to discover, understand and live by God's boundaries.

Chapter 4: Created for Community

1. Define *harmony*.
2. List a few reasons why harmony is attractive or desirable.
3. Discuss how the life, ministry and sacrifice of Christ give us a picture of who God is and the harmony he longs for in our lives and relationship with him.
4. Describe how/why confession is an important step toward healing our relationship with others and God.
5. Discuss how confession leads to healing, restored community, and a life of love.
6. *Challenge:* We don't value harmony or connections with others when we refuse to recognize and confess the wrongs we have participated in which hurt others and cause separation.
7. *Next Steps*: (1) identify someone you value or who has blessed you and write them expressing gratitude and thanks; (2) identify someone you've hurt; write them admitting wrong and ask for forgiveness; (3) identify someone you need to repair relationship with, set up a private, face-to-face meeting, share your regret, and ask for forgiveness.
8. Discuss the value of these steps of restoring harmony and healing.

Chapter 5: The Birth of the ME Addiction

1. Define *temptation*.
2. List several of what you would consider to be life's most tempting wrongs or sins.
3. Identify/discuss why tempting things are so . . . tempting!
4. Discuss the role of God's word, relationships with godly people, and prayer in helping us resist temptation.
5. Describe some of the general ways sin habits or addictions form in our lives.

6. Describe how it is possible to train our bodies to be godly instead of suckers for temptation.

7. Describe/list some of the spiritual disciplines that we might use to help us resist temptation.

8. *Challenge*: We want what we want and we can become experts of describing the things we desire, feel we need or believe would gratify us! Temptation is the state of letting the desires of our body direct our life decisions. We need to get over ourselves! In order to pursue a total mind-and-heart makeover, we need to say *yes* to God-glorifying, Jesus-first and Holy Spirit-filled events, practices and activities. Daily!

9. *Next Steps*: Identify then describe something you can and will add to your daily/weekly life that refocuses your mind and heart toward God.

Chapter 6: A ME-Sized Appetite

1. Describe/define *guilty pleasure*.

2. Discuss whether you agree with this principal: "What you give your attention to and focus most upon is what you will grow to value and desire more than anything else."

3. Contrast/describe the difference between need and want.

4. Describe some of the emotional or intellectual steps when progressing from need to craving to obsession.

5. Discuss why desires and cravings often lead us into bad or selfish decisions.

6. Discuss/describe the harm unhealthy addictions have on our faith.

7. *Challenge*: Sin is an addiction we cannot possibly defeat on our own. We need God's grace and God's power if we are going to identify and give up centering our hearts on personal comfort, unhealthy desires and faith crushing cravings!

8. *Next Steps*: (1) identify unhealthy cravings, obsessions or addictions in your life; (2) describe ways these cravings negatively affect your faith; (3) identify a faith-supporting friend who can help you address these unhealthy cravings; (4) with

your faith-supporting friend's help, devise reasonable, doable strategies for dealing with these cravings; (5) set up regular times of face-to-face prayer with your supporting friend to ask for God's help to empower removal of these cravings.

9. Describe how activating these steps could help curb your unhealthy self-focused appetites.

Chapter 7: ME-nough

1. Define *covet*.
2. Discuss/identify the processes involved in our thoughts when a want moves from being just a distraction to becoming a craving.
3. Identify and describe decisions or attitudes that change a simple desire into the action of going and doing something.
4. Discuss the connection between craving, obsession and addiction . . . to worry, anxiety, and guilt.
5. Discuss/describe what is involved with placing one noble or essential goal over and above every other want or need in life.
6. Discuss what it means practically to place Christ first in our lives.
7. *Challenge: Living with a Jesus-focused faith* is essentially a discipline. We discipline ourselves to value faith, to put desires that glorify God first, and to place ourselves second even when we don't really want to. We choose, over and over and over again, to let conviction guide our behavior, not craving. Conviction is a faith discipline fueled by prayer, the study of God's word, and a life lived in spiritual community. Faith conviction is the foundation for a growing relationship with God which can and will reorient our life focus and experience. Are you ready for your faith to move from a focus on yourself to a focus wholly on God? Really?
8. *Next Steps:* Describe one or two noble or essential spiritual goals for your life that you believe God wants to empower over and above every other want or need in your life.

Chapter 8: The ME-ego

1. Define and give some examples of the negative meaning of the word *ego*.
2. Describe the difference between positive ambition and selfish ego.
3. Discuss/identify some of the roots of pride.
4. Describe how pride erodes and damages our faith and relationship with God.
5. Define *selfless sacrifice*.
6. Identify and contrast the motivation behind, and resulting fruit differences between, prideful religious acts and selfless service.
7. Discuss how selfless service helps guard our hearts against pride.
8. *Challenge:* You cannot displace an unhealthy focus on yourself by just sitting there wishing you weren't so self-absorbed. Get up and serve somebody! True service is an act of sacrificial love. You get over yourself by giving up time, energy and money to sacrificially serve and love others. The addiction to self begins to die a little every time we put our desires second and the needs of others first.
9. *Next Steps*: (1) spend the next twenty-four hours watching for and listing any and all needs you become aware of in your local community, church or the world; (2) in a group or with a faith supporting friend, pray, asking God, who, what, and how to serve; (3) after a service target is identified, research appropriate ways to partner with others to serve this target; (4) do it; (5) do it again!
10. Describe any concerns, fears, or hesitations involved with taking these next steps.
11. Reflection: What change(s) is the Holy Spirit working in you as you implement the steps in item 9, above?

Chapter 9: Excuse ME

1. Define and give examples of the negative meaning of excuses.

2. Identify and discuss negative ways an excuse impacts our relationship with God and others.
3. Discuss how an excuse is connected with placing blame on others.
4. Describe how mature faith involves accepting blame for our sin before we take it to the blood of Jesus.
5. Discuss how confessing our sin encourages our dependency upon and trust in God.
6. Discuss how confessing our sin discourages or helps heal us from the ME-addiction.
7. *Challenge*: An excuse brings hurt to others or God by passing the blame for our behavior or decisions. This puts the focus on protecting ourselves instead of trusting God or blessing others. Offering excuses is an insidious, harmful disease that must be forcefully cut out of our lives. It is also a telltale symptom of the ME-virus. Until we root out and destroy excuses and blame-casting from our lives, we cannot begin to be free from the ME-addiction!
8. *Next Steps*: (1) identify excuses and areas of your life where you are tempted to blame others for mistakes or pain you feel; (2) pray for the strength to resist the temptation to excuse your decisions or blame others. (3) make amends for any excuse making or blame casting in your recent past; (4) ask your faith-supporting friend to help you consistently and publicly confess wrongs you have committed and demonstrate trust in God's grace.
9. Discuss the value in making these next steps happen in your life.

Chapter 10: Find ME

1. Describe why we're embarrassed about things from our life or past and hide them from others.
2. Discuss how hidden embarrassment or secret things bring pain, wounds or fear into our lives.
3. Describe how secrecy impacts our relationship with God.

4. List things you or others try to keep secret.
5. Describe reasons and excuses for hiding or keeping fears, wounds and sins secret.
6. *Challenge*: There is no such thing as a secret from God. Our faith and trust is held captive by our inability to be open to God and others about our mistakes, fears and wounds. We cannot beat a sin we do not openly admit to and ask help for in defeating. Secret sin is the breeding ground for a self-absorbed, self-addicted heart.
7. *Next Steps*: It's time to run to God by writing down your secrets and asking God to help you confess them to someone you can trust who will encourage your faith and pray for your healing.
8. Describe any concerns you have with admitting your secrets.

Chapter 11: ME & Family

1. Anger and jealousy were the first sins that brought rage, family grief and murder into the world. Describe some of the ways anger and jealousy have hurt you or those you know.
2. Cain sulked away from others while nurturing a spirit of anger and jealousy. Discuss what God meant when he warned Cain that sin wanted to own him.
3. Anger and jealousy block out reasonable thinking and healthy interactions with others. Describe how anger and sin make feeling accepted and loved by God next to impossible.
4. The way anger and jealousy work in us demonstrates how the ME-addiction works as well. Discuss how the ME-addiction is connected to a desire for acceptance and love.
5. When we are angry, jealous, or feel wounded by others, we are tempted to withdraw like Cain. Describe some situations, challenges, or relationships where you see anger or jealously working in your life.
6. *Challenge*: God wants to displace the ME-addiction with the presence of his Spirit. But you cannot become full of the Spirit when your heart is already full of yourself. It is time to starve

the addiction of ME by feeding the Spirit of thee. As the Holy Spirit increases in your life, he always aims you toward the truth of God's love and gifts for your life.

7. *Next Steps*: (1) recover the facts of God's acceptance of you by deepening your understanding of the truth of that love in Scripture; (2) recover the facts of God's acceptance of you by asking faith friends to pray over you, asking God to strengthen your affection for Him while weakening your addiction to yourself; (3) reconnect to opportunities to serve others, sharing God's love and message through acts of love; (4) devote part of each day to nurturing faith in study of the Word, prayer, and service to others.

8. Discuss how taking these next steps can help you overcome your ME-addiction.

Chapter 12: Living ME-Free

1. All of us have a ME-addiction. How would you describe evidence from your life that demonstrates your ME-addiction?

2. Change comes when we come face-to-face with who we really are. Discuss the power of identifying and confessing some of the ME-addicted lifestyles or attitudes evident in your life.

3. Transformation of our character, preferences, and desires is a gift of God. Describe some of the tools or ways you think God will use to help you break free of your ME-addiction.

4. Jesus is the perfect image of who we want to become. List some of the character traits of Jesus you feel God most desires to develop in your life and contrast them with the "ME-addicted" character traits now at work in you:

Jesus character traits vs. ME-addicted character traits

5. *Challenge*: We can help God in changing our character ... but we can't do it all by ourselves. The transformation is the work and gift of God. Will you commit to partner with God in initiating and continuing this work of transformation in your life?

6. *Next Steps*: Identify the most important spiritual tools critical for God's transforming work in your life. The Word, prayer, fasting, fellowship, removing things, adding things, radical change, subtle changes . . . and note them here:

    _____.

    Then discuss these next steps with your share or prayer group.

Chapter 13: Breaking Free from the Kingdom of ME

1. Living in the kingdom of God is very different from living in the kingdom of ME. How would you describe some of the differences between the two?
2. Citizens of the kingdom of God live focused on fulfilling the wishes and will of their king. Describe a few of the wishes and will of God for our lives.
3. You have a great reason for being and purpose in the kingdom of God. Discuss the purposes each of us has in God's kingdom when we live to fulfill God's wishes and will.
4. The kingdom of ME is on a collision course with the kingdom of God. Describe evidences you see of this conflict or collision going on in your life or in the lives of those you know.
5. *Challenge*: The essence of the ME-addiction is a choice about who is going to rule your life: You or God. Your desires or God's eternal plans. Your fear or God's promises. Your endless need to be gratified or God's endless ability to provide what you truly need. When we fully submit to God as king, our trust relies only on God's provision in life or in death. To trust and follow God as king is to relinquish everything—even the right to be afraid. Are you ready to crown God as king even over your desire to complain?
6. *Next Steps*: Discuss your fears, resistance, or reluctance to fully submitting all of your life to God as king and ruler of your life.

Endnotes

Chapter 1: A ME-free World

1. Genesis 1:1
2. Ibid.
3. Genesis 1:2
4. Genesis 2:8-9
5. See Revelation 21 and 22

Chapter 2: The Reason for Being

1. Gene Weingarten, "Pearls Before Breakfast: Can one of the nation's great musicians cut through the fog of a D.C. rush hour? Let's find out," Sunday, April 8, 2007, www.washingtonpost.com/wp-dyn/content/article/2007/04/04/AR2007040401721.html.
2. Genesis 3:8
3. Genesis 2:16-17
4. Genesis 3:6
5. Jeremiah 17:9
6. Mark 1:35
7. Mark Galli, "A Rustling in the Garden: Why we sometimes wish the atheists were right," *Christianity Today*, November 29, 2007, www.christianitytoday.com/ct/2007/novemberweb-only/148-42.0.html?start=2.
8. Hebrews 4:15-16

9. See Andrew Newberg, MD. and Mark Robert Waldman, *How God Changes Your Brain: Breakthrough Findings from a Leading Neuroscientist,* at www.andrewnewberg.com/change.asp for a short synopsis.
10. See Psalm 1 and Psalm 119:97
11. Romans 12:1

Chapter 3: A World With Boundaries

1. Genesis 2:15
2. Genesis 2:16
3. 1 Corinthians 6:12
4. Ibid.
5. Genesis 2:17
6. "Tareq And Michaele Salahi: White House Party Crashers Walk Into State Dinner, Put Arm Around Joe Biden," www.huffingtonpost.com/2009/11/25/tareq-and-michaele-salahi_n_371336.html?view=print.
7. A helpful discussion is found with Dallas Willard at www.mppc.org/toughquestions.
8. Jeremiah 29:13

Chapter 4: Created for Community

1. Colossians 1:15
2. Hebrews 1:3
3. For more on perichoresis see Shirley C. Guthrie, *Christian Doctrine* (Westminster/John Knox Press: Louisville, Kentucky, 1994), 91–5.
4. See Genesis 2:23
5. Genesis 2:18
6. John 13:34–35
7. Dave Ferguson,_*The Big Idea* (Zondervan: Grand Rapids, Michigan, 2007), 48–50.
8. Romans 12:10
9. Romans 12:15

10. Romans 15:7
11. Romans 16:16
12. 1 Corinthians 1:10
13. Colossians 3:13
14. Ephesians 5:19
15. Colossians 3:16
16. Hebrews 10:25
17. From Calvin Miller on the *Be Still* DVD series found at www. bestillprayer.com/?content=calvin&video=true.

Chapter 5: The Birth of the ME Addiction

1. Genesis 2:25
2. Genesis 3:1
3. Genesis 2:16-17
4. Genesis 3:2
5. Genesis 3:4-5
6. Genesis 5:5
7. Romans 7:23
8. C.S. Lewis, *The Screwtape Letters and Screwtape Proposes a Toast* (New York: MacMillan, 1962), 11.
9. See Romans 3:23, 26 and Romans 5:12
10. Romans 6:11
11. Romans 6:13
12. 1 Timothy 4:7
13. Dallas Willard, *The Spirit of the Disciplines*, (San Francisco: Harper & Row, 1988), 101.

Chapter 6: A ME Sized Appetite

1. Genesis 3:1
2. Genesis 3:6
3. 1 John 2:15-16
4. Luke 22:15
5. Philippians 1:23-24
6. 1 Thessalonians 2:17

7. Romans 13:14
8. Galatians 5:16
9. United States Department of Agriculture, *Profiling Food Consumption in America,* www.usda.gov/factbook/chapter2.htm.
10. John 4:32
11. John 4:34
12. Psalm 23:1-3

Chapter 7: ME nough

1. William Poundstone, "Maddest of the 'Mad Men:' The 'Mad Man' behind the subliminal advertising controversy," *Priceless,* January 17, 2010, www.psychologytoday.com/blog/priceless/201001/maddest-the-mad-men.
2. Genesis 3:1
3. Genesis 3:2
4. 2 Samuel 11:1-5
5. Mark 9:47
6. Jean Kilbourne, "Jesus is a Brand of Jeans," *New Internationalist Magazine,* September 1, 2006, www.newint.org/features/2006/09/01/culture/.
7. Exodus 20:17
8. Matthew 6:25-32
9. Matthew 6:33
10. Psalm 23:1
11. Kilbourne.
12. Alison Motluk, "Subliminal advertising may work afterall," *NewScientist,* April 28, 2006, www.newscientist.com/article/mg19025494.400-subliminal-advertising-may-work-after-all.html.
13. Matthew 13:44

Chapter 8: ME ego

1. Proverbs 16:18
2. www.civilwarbattlefields.us/spotsylvania/sedgwick.html.

3. Genesis 2:17
4. Exodus 20:8
5. Proverbs 6:6
6. Proverbs 22:7; Hebrews 13:5-6
7. Colossians 3:5-9
8. Proverbs 16:5
9. Proverbs 8:13
10. Proverbs 6:16-17
11. Luke 12:16-20
12. Proverbs 18:12
13. Proverbs 21:4
14. *Distinguishing Marks*, in works of Jonathan Edwards, Volume 4, Great Awakening, ed. C. C. Goen (New Haven Yale University Press, 1970), 277-78, www.edwards.yale.edu/archive?path=aHR 0cDovL2Vkd2FyZHMueWFsZS5lZHUvY2dpLWJpbi9uZX dwaGlsby9nZXRvYmplY3QucGw/Yy4zOjUud2plbw==.
15. 1 Corinthians 4:3-4

Chapter 9: Excuse ME

1. Some of you younger readers will need to stop right now, Google Apple II computer, look at the image, and laugh. Then return to your reading.
2. Anick Jesdanun, "First PC virus relatively tame / Practical joke 25 years ago harmless compared to attacks that followed," Houston Chronicle, September 1, 2007, www.chron.com/ CDS/archives/archive.mpl?id=2007_4416057.
3. Ibid.
4. Genesis 2:15
5. Genesis 3:17-19
6. Genesis 2:17
7. Genesis 3:5
8. Jesdanun.
9. Genesis 3:12
10. Genesis 3:13
11. Found at www.gomilpitas.com/humor/108.htm.

12. www.quotegarden.com/excuses.html.
13. www.ahajokes.com/fp016.html.
14. See Romans 5:12ff.
15. Romans 5:19
16. Hebrews 5:8
17. James 5:16

Chapter 10: Find ME

1. Scott Semegran, "20 Questions with Frank Warren," *Quirkee. com*, Thursday, August 3, 2006, www.quirkee.com/content/ view/148/46/.
2. "Interview with Frank Warren, founder of PostSecret.com, Part One," BerksTV.com, 2006 accessed 6 Feb. 2007, www.berks. tv/interview-with-frank-warren-founder-of-postsecretcom-part-one/.
3. Ibid.
4. Ibid., "20 Questions with Frank Warren."
5. Genesis 3:8-10
6. Genesis 3:7
7. Genesis 2:25
8. Genesis 3:10-13
9. www.annoyingstuff.com/category/crimes/stupid-criminals/.
10. Genesis 3:21
11. Luke 15:11-32
12. 1 John 1:8-9
13. James 5:16
14. Galatians 3:26

Chapter 11: ME & Family

1. Genesis 2:15
2. Genesis 4:3
3. Genesis 4:4
4. Genesis1:28
5. Genesis 4:7

6. Michelle Koidin, "'Cheerleader Mom' freed after serving six months," *Abilene Reporter News*, March 1, 1997, www.texnews.com/texas97/mom030197.html.
7. Mike Celizic, "Tonya Harding reveals her side of 'roller coaster life,'" *Today*, May 15, 2008, http://today.msnbc.msn.com/id/24645352/ns/today-today_people/t/tonya-harding-reveals-her—side-roller-coaster-life/.
8. Genesis 4:9
9. Romans 12:9-10
10. James 4:1

Chapter 12: Living ME-free

1. Exodus 34:29
2. Mark 9:2-3
3. Acts 6:5
4. Acts 6:15
5. 2 Corinthians 3:18
6. Real person but not his real name.
7. John 21:9
8. John 21:22
9. Nathaniel Hawthorn, *The Great Stone Face*, www.classicreader.com/book/726/1/.

Chapter 13: Breaking Free from the Kingdom of ME

1. See Republic of Molossia Official Website at www.molossia.org for more of the story.
2. Mark 1:15
3. 1 Samuel 12:12
4. Daniel 4:34
5. Jeremiah 32:39
6. Micah 5:2
7. Mark 4:3-8
8. Mark 4:9
9. Matthew 6:9-10

10. Matthew 28:18

Afterword: The ME–Free Revolution

1. Jim Henderson and Matt Casper, *Jim and Casper Go to Church: Frank Conversation about Faith, Churches, and Well-Meaning Christians,* (Carol Stream, Illinois: Tyndale House Publishers, Inc., 2007).
2. *An Interview with Pastor Jim Henderson and Atheist Matt Casper,* www.sermoncentral.com/ article. asp?article=a-Henderson_Casper_05_28_07&ac=true.
3. Like that word? Just made it up.
4. Bono, "This Generation's Moonshot," Time Magazine, Tuesday, November 1, 2005, www.time.com/time/magazine/article/0,9171,1124333,00.html.
5. World Vision, *About Hunger, Hunger Facts,* www.worldvision.org/content.nsf/learn/hunger-facts?Open&lpos=lft_txt_Hunger-Facts.
6. See organizations like www.worldvision.org or http://www.compassion.com/ to learn more.
7. Peter Warski, "Hard Facts About Labor Trafficking," *World Vision,* blog.worldvision.org/causes/hard-facts-about-labor-trafficking/?open&lpos=day_txt_ trafficking-blog.
8. U.S. Department of Justice, *Child Prostitution,* www.justice.gov/criminal/ceos/ prostitution.html.
9. Malaria No More, *About Malaria,* www.malarianomore.org/malaria.
10. Living Water International, *A Global Crisis,* www.water.cc/water-crisis/.
11. Stand for Africa, *What Can a Dollar Do?,* www.standforafrica.org/.
12. Wolfgang Saxon, "Rev. John Stott, Major Evangelical Figure, Dies at 90," *The New York Times,* July 27, 2011, www.nytimes.com/2011/07/28/world/europe/28stott.html?_r=1&ref=obituaries.

About the ME Addiction Team

Rick Brown is the lead pastor of ChristBridge Fellowship in Tomball, Texas, in the Houston area since 1999. His church's mission to "impact the community for eternity" has led him and others to become involved in councils and boards and service groups to help make the city a better place for everyone. Rick has been married to Karen since 1986 and they have two sons—Kristofer and Taylor—and one daughter-in-law, Jenn.

Reg Cox has ministered in the Denver, Colorado area since 2002. He has spoken extensively for teen—and college-age groups and led spiritual renewal events throughout the nation and world. He is married to Amy and they have one son, Levi, and one daughter, Faith.

Jer Villanueva has ministered in Seattle, Washington, and Northern California since 1994. He enjoys teaching and seeing others transformed in Christ. He holds a master of science in Ministry and master of divinity from Pepperdine University. He is married to Lyn and they have three children: Sydney, Elias, and Noelle.

Dr. Glen Villanueva is a family physician serving the underserved in Modesto, California since 1997. As Co-founder of Shoestring Ministries, he is able to fulfill his passion to help heal the physically sick and minister to the soul. Glen is married to Yvonne and they have two daughters, Maya and Ani.

CPSIA information can be obtained at www.ICGtesting.com
Printed in the USA
BVOW042346011211

277282BV00002B/3/P